Camping Therapy

CAMPING THERAPY

Its Uses in Psychiatry and Rehabilitation

Edited by

THOMAS POWER LOWRY, M.D., F.A.P.A.
Lecturer, Center for Training in Community Psychiatry
Berkeley, California
Formerly Director, Division of Mental Health
New Mexico Department of Hospitals and Institutions

WITH SEVENTEEN ADDITIONAL CONTRIBUTORS

With a Foreword by

Richard W. Hudgens, M.D.
Associate Professor of Psychiatry
Associate Dean
Washington University School of Medicine
St. Louis, Missouri

CHARLES C THOMAS • PUBLISHER
Springfield • Illinois • U.S.A.

Published and Distributed Throughout the World by

CHARLES C THOMAS • PUBLISHER
Bannerstone House
301-327 East Lawrence Avenue, Springfield, Illinois, U.S.A.

ISBN 0-398-02898-2

Library of Congress Catalog Card Number: 73-10082

With THOMAS BOOKS careful attention is given to all details of manufacturing and design. It is the Publisher's desire to present books that are satisfactory as to their physical qualities and artistic possibilities and appropriate for their particular use. THOMAS BOOKS will be true to those laws of quality that assure a good name and good will.

Printed in the United States of America
C-1

Library of Congress Cataloging in Publication Data

Lowry, Thomas P.
Camping therapy.

Includes bibliographical references.
1. Recreational therapy—Addresses, essays, lectures.
2. Camping—Addresses, essays, lectures. I. Title.
[DNLM: 1. Camping. 2. Mental disorders—Therapy.
WM450 L921c 1973]
RC489.R4L68 616.8'916'5 73-10082
ISBN 0-398-02898-2

CONTRIBUTORS

ORA K. ACKERMAN, M.Ed.
Coordinator of Activity Therapies, Evansville State Hospital
Evansville, Indiana

RUTH B. CAPLAN, M.A.
Associate in Psychiatry, Harvard Medical School
Boston, Massachusetts

NORMAN FLAX, M.S.W., Ph.D.
Research Associate, Washington University, St. Louis, Missouri
Director of Research, Jewish Community Centers Association

LOIS GOODRICH
Executive Director, Trail Blazer Camps (formerly Life Camps)
New York, New York

DR. ERNEST HARMS
Child Psychologist
New York, New York

TOM R. HOBBS, M.A.
Clinical Psychometrist
Bureau of Mental Health
Birmingham, Alabama

HENRY K. KAPLAN, Ph.D.
Clinical Psychologist
Mendota State Hospital
Madison, Wisconsin

DELBERT M. KOLE, M.D.
Coordinator for Project Development
Oregon Regional Medical Program
Portland, Oregon

MARGARET C. McDONALD
Production Coordinator
PSYCHIATRIC NEWS
Washington, D.C.

FRANCES W. McFARLAND, M.A.
Clinical Psychologist
Stockton State Hospital
Stockton, California

FRITZ REDL, Ph.D.
Professor of Behavioral Sciences
Wayne State University
Detroit, Michigan

E. EDWARD REITMAN, Ph.D.
Director, Day Treatment Center
Houston Veterans Administration Hospital
Houston, Texas

ELIZABETH MARY REMAR
Chief, Volunteer Services
Department of Mental Health
Commonwealth of Massachusetts
Boston, Massachusetts

BERT KRUGER SMITH
The Hogg Foundation for Mental Health
University of Texas
Austin, Texas

JOHN EDWARD TALLEY, M.D.
Jungian Analyst
Santa Fe, New Mexico

MAXWELL N. WEISMAN, M.D.
Director, Division of Alcoholism Control
Maryland Department of Health and Mental Hygiene
Baltimore, Maryland

RUTH G. WHITTEKIN, B.S.
Recreation Therapist
Veterans Administration Hospital
Waco, Texas

FOREWORD

Paraphrasing Winston Churchill's remark about Clement Attlee: *Workers in the field of mental health have much to be modest about.*

We know too little about the origins, mechanisms, and proper treatment of the disorders we are asked to alleviate, whether these are disorders of brain structure and function or disorders springing from disruptive life experiences. And as a group, we psychiatrists, psychologists, social workers, activity therapists, nurses, counsellors, and so forth, fall short when it comes to the practical application even of that knowledge we do possess. This state of affairs is bad enough as it is, but too many people in the field have made the situation worse by laying claim to more knowledge than they possess and by reporting cures they have not wrought. It is refreshing, then, to read a book which makes no immodest claims and which presents in down-to-earth language the theory and practical applications under various conditions of an important type of therapy. As these chapters indicate, camping therapy is applicable not only for selected psychiatric patients of all types, but for people who have received no label as mentally ill or emotionally disturbed; it is a therapy which can be the primary form of treatment or adjunctive to other forms of treatment, enhancing their effectiveness.

In these pages the seventeen contributors describe a broad range of experience. Extensive and thoughtful work has been done with young people who are well, adolescents with delinquent behavior, people ill with depression, schizophrenia and other syndromes, short-term psychiatric hospital patients, and people who have been institutionalized for many years. The reader of this book will become aware that camping therapy is a field with a specific body of knowledge, comprising among other things understanding of group processes and of proper selection of staff and campers, as well as of the ancient, traditional techniques of camping itself. Nowhere in this book is camping therapy proclaimed as a panacea for human unhappiness or for psychiatric disorders. It is a form of treatment which does not compete with other forms of treatment, whether they are individual counselling, group psychotherapy, the somatic therapies, or *what have you.* Frustrations as well as triumphs are detailed here, and pitfalls to be avoided are discussed along with guides to success. The book can not only serve to open the eyes of mental health professionals to a field with which they may not be familiar; it is also a practical guide to the implementation of camping therapy programs. In addition, the selected references in the chapters and appendix provide ample additional information, both of the theoretical and *how to do it* type.

Dr. Thomas Lowry, the editor of this book, is an unusual psychiatrist. He has broad interests and has pursued each of them in depth, with scholarly research and personal commitment. Thus during his career he has equipped himself to help people with a great variety of problems, ranging from troubled marriages to severe psychoses, and to use varied approaches applicable to the people he is helping and the ailments afflicting them. In the twelve years I have known him Dr. Lowry has never had the comfortable delusion that he knows enough to stop looking for better ways to treat patients, nor has he been rigid or doctrinaire. In harmony with his approach to psychiatry, this book tells a lot about one way mental health professionals may help to free people for a fuller life, whether their approach to patients is through a medical, social, or individual model, or a combination of the three. Camping therapy offers one road to the goal of all therapies, expressed in the Navajo healing chant quoted in Dr. Talley's chapter: "The world before me is restored in beauty."

RICHARD W. HUDGENS, M.D.

PREFACE

To your tents, O Israel. I. Kings XII:16.

EVERY BOOK, no matter how technical, is in some way a personal statement of the author and his reflection of all who have influenced him. My contact with camping began two generations ago when my grandfather, Dr. Henry Power, took my mother on extended camping trips to Idaho and eastern Washington, long before the advent of campgrounds and recreational vehicles. When I was age four, my grandmother took me on my first contact with the wilderness: a summer cattle drive in the heavy timber of California's rugged Mendocino Coast, still today the last stretch of United States coastline without a major road. A few years later, my family and I spent several summers at the Sierra Nevada log cabin of my godfather, Francis Cross. This vast, dark, handhewn cabin, built by his father, reeked with the rich aroma of fifty years of woodsmoke, slightly damp Navajo blankets and old books relegated to summer reading. A hand cranked phonograph and a collection of boats in various states of disrepair gave wings to summer days.

From that cabin, I accompanied my parents and brother on my first overnight camping trip, to Lake of the Woods. The pleasure and sense of mystery of being away from civilization is no surprise to any experienced camper, but must be experienced rather than heard about secondhand.

My long and pleasant association with the Boy Scouts began in the San Joaquin Valley. Our Scoutmaster, Tom Yancey, took us to Oso Canyon in the California coast range, where we learned to cook without tools. During the following eight years, I was at first a camper and later a counselor at Camp Wallace

Alexander in California's Feather River Canyon. The experience and responsibility of leading long backpacking expeditions into the High Sierras was an important part of my maturation. Though I learned from many people those summers, my most consistent debt is to Henry Blaylock, who was Scout Executive for the Piedmont Council.

The years of college, medical school, residency training and Air Force raced by with precious few opportunities for camping. When I became Director of the Psychiatric Section of Ross General Hospital in California, I had an opportunity to encourage the use of camping as a therapeutic modality with a variety of patients many of whom were psychotic. The success of this program, described in a later chapter, would not have been possible without the understanding and encouragement of the hospital's administrator, Dr. John C. Siemens, and of Carole Kinney and Joan Cline of our Nursing and Occupational Therapy Staff. This program was nominated for an American Psychiatric Association Hospital Achievement Award.

In 1969, I became Director of Psychiatry at New Mexico State Hospital and reintroduced a program of summer camps, which had been discontinued by one of my predecessors. Dozens of staff and volunteers labored to make these programs a success; I have special gratitude for the hospital administrator, Leonard A. Nuckolls, who found ways of doing things without money and Bennie J. Sanders and Nicholas H. Hashey, whose skills as camp directors were visible night and day.

Medical writing comes most easily with the help of a good librarian. I have special gratitude for Julie Schmidt and Hazel Hurley, directors of the medical libraries at Marin General Hospital and New Mexico State Hospital, respectively.

As a testimony of my own, I offer the following experience. Several years ago, during a period of profound change in my life, I had been camping alone for several days in Desolation Valley Wilderness Area in the Sierra Nevada, during a rainy September. I had been up most of the night, attempting to keep dry; during a long lull in the rain and wind I noticed, behind the silence, an extremely low pitched hum. It was certainly not any distant highway or passing jet airplane, nor was it the wind in the trees. While not at all obtrusive, this deep and constant tone could be readily heard with the slightest focusing of attention. I have no explanation for it, but cannot avoid thinking of the final chapter of Hermann Hesse's *Siddhartha.* The hero has been listening to the many voices of the river; at last, he hears them mingle into one note.

> All of them together was the stream of events, the music of life. When Siddhartha listened attentively to this river, to this song of a thousand voices; when he did not listen to the sorrow or laughter, when he did not bind his soul to any one particular voice and absorb it in his Self, but heard them all, the whole, the unity; then the great song of a thousand voices consisted of one word: Om—perfection.

Siddhartha and his teacher both began to smile radiantly.

> His wound was healing, his pain was dispersing; his Self had merged into Unity.

THOMAS P. LOWRY, M.D.

INTRODUCTION

One impulse from a vernal wood
May teach you more of man,
Of moral evil and of good,
Than all the sages can.
The Tables Turned,
William Wordsworth

THE USE OF CAMPING as a means of rehabilitation in mental illness is by no means new, and has roots in one of the most powerful and recurrent themes in philosophy.

That theme is the Myth of the Golden Age, known to students of English literature as Chronological Primitivism, the belief that the life and actions of man were more admirable and desirable at an earlier stage of history than at present. Dreamers and theorists of every stripe, describe a Paradise Lost, free from toil and from grief. This illusion, that health and happiness are within man's possibilities, and obtainable by the simple life, has flourished in many different forms throughout history. In the Old Testament, the Patriarchs are said to have lived hundreds of years. The ancient Greeks believed in the existence of happy races, filled with vigor and virtue, in inaccessible parts of the earth. In 400 B.C., the Yellow Emperor in his *Classic of Internal Medicine,* stated that in times even more ancient, that men lived to a great age and maintained their vigor and health. This age of harmony eventually drew to a close, for reasons not entirely clear; the ensuing lack of harmony opened men to illness.*

The logical development from these beliefs is an attempt at

* Veith, Ilza: *The Yellow Emperor's Classic of Internal Medicine.* Berkeley, University of California Press, 1966.

the return to nature. During the eighteenth century, the most vocal proponent of this gospel was Jean Jacques Rousseau, who asserted that man in his natural state was happy, healthy and virtuous; man's troubles derived from the spoiling and corruption brought by civilization. Rousseau imagined that the ideal man was the savage, untainted by civilization. His deadliest enemy, Voltaire, derided these primitivistic notions in his book, *L'Ingenue,* which described the behavior of a Huron Indian in France. This fictional Indian is natural enough and the uninhibited play of his appetites and instincts lead to embarrassing situations in the salons of Europe. The unreality of the return to nature movement was best seen in the absurd but charming hamlet built by Marie Antoinette on the edge of the park of Versailles, where powdered marchionesses played with her at haymaking and tending cows, pretending to experience the idyllic simplicity of rustic life.

These ideas of simple, outdoor living are far from dead. The history of American applied philosophy includes such individual attempts at naturalism as Thoreau's *Walden,* and the many group attempts which are part of the long history of the American commune movement. Since the exploration of the South Seas, the natives of Polynesia were most frequently cited as proving the virtues of the simple life. The greatest praise was generally given by the explorer with the least anthropological knowledge, but even today the allure of the tropics attracts herds of tourists to the hotels of Honolulu which, of course, are no more a return to nature than Marie Antoinette's play farm.

The influence of these notions upon medical theory is delightfully detailed by Rene Dubos,* who considers the whole sweep of history as he contrasts the fantasies and realities of man's search for health and philosophic balance. In Christian mythology, the original Golden Age was, of course, the Garden of Eden from which Adam and Eve were expelled. In contemporary life, our wishes to restore such natural living are reflected in many institutions: country clubs, hunting lodges, ski chalets, beach bungalows, moonlight clambakes, nudist colonies, backyard barbe-

* Dubos, Rene: *The Mirage of Health.* New York, Harper, 1959.

ques in suburban gardens and the numerous nature cults extolling the virtues of wind, sun, bitter vegetable juices, coarse food and the careful collection of rotting leaves.

A political ramification of these beliefs is seen in many states, where a rural controlled legislature declines to come to the aid of their rotting cities, based upon almost inarticulate, but strongly held, beliefs that city folks have deliberately chosen a life which is overcomplex, effete, degenerate, and somehow undeserving of sympathy. This feeling influenced the previous policy of building mental hospitals out in the country, which served the purposes of exposing the patients to beneficial fresh air and extensive gardening, as well as getting them out of sight. A valuable examination of this problem was recently made by Srole,* who takes up the question of the influence of rural life on mental health. He concludes that the traditional question has really been placed upside down and rather than ask what effects do community differences exert on the mental health of their inhabitants, we should ask what kind of people differentially stay in or are drawn to various kinds of communities? Having lived in close proximity to both urban and rural slums, I find myself in complete agreement with his conclusions that, in general, both urban and rural slums are more psychopathogenic than are nonslum neighborhoods and that, for adults seeking a change in environment, the city is a more therapeutic milieu than the small community, especially for the many troubled deviants who cannot stand being highly visible. Thus, the twin ideas of Return to Nature and City as Destroying Temptress are both myths.

It seems and feels clear to the author that living at home in a city, and living in some wilderness environment, with opportunities for physical challenge, are different experiences. Whether it is some inherent virtue in the outdoors or whether it is a matter of contrast, my colleagues and I who have attempted to employ therapeutic camping experiences, see behavior changes in patients, which appear to be significant and are confirmed by the reports of the patients themselves. At this point, there is hardly any evidence to clarify cause and effect and it is quite possible

* Srole, Leo: Urbanization and mental health—some reformulations. *Am. Sci.*, *60*:576, 1972.

that camping therapy, like many other beneficial maneuvers, is simply a variant of the Hawthorne effect, in which almost any change made in a social system produces benefit, simply by virtue of the attention to the recipient and the apparent intentions of the doer.

The camping movement in America during the first half of this century encompassed two major areas: *character building* influences for normal campers and therapeutic influences for the *abnormal.* Probably the classic book for the former is *Camping and Character,** which describes the philosophy and functioning of Camp Ahmek. The authors devote three hundred pages to describing the methods and virtues of their approach to an organized camping program, and then summarize their attempts to measure behavioral change, both within the camp and in the period after the children returned to their homes. Somewhat sadly they concluded that, "probably the effectiveness of the summer camp in developing desirable social attitudes and behavior is much below the customary expectation." They also concluded that the counselor that works the closest with the campers is far more important than any director or professional, that the amount of favorable change decreases with increasing age and that parents are more optimistic in rating improvements than are the camp leaders.

Dr. Ernest Harms, a senior child psychologist, for many years has worked to bring European and American concepts of therapeutic camping into closer harmony. During his editorship of *The Nervous Child,* an entire issue was devoted to the mental health aspects of camping, especially for children who were moderately deviant in their behavior. For the severely disturbed, camping therapy had its origin in Tent Therapy, whose origin almost a century ago is well described in Ruth Caplan's chapter.

Many approaches to camping therapy are seen in other chapters of this book. A wide variety of patient groups, therapeutic rationales, approaches to financing, innovation in staffing patterns and choice of settings is evident. Readers interested in uti-

---

* Dimock, Hedley S., and Hendry, Charles E.: *Camping and Character.* New York, Association Press, 1929.

lizing camping therapy are likely to find among these descriptions something usefully adaptable to their own setting.

My own preference is for programs which use as little as possible in the way of fixed equipment (i.e. cabins, kitchens, playgrounds), and rely more upon small group activity, especially that centering around necessities of survival, such as providing a comfortable place to sleep, the gathering of wood, the preparation of food and the helping of one another in these tasks.

In an institution like a chronic mental hospital, *it really doesn't make any difference whether the patient does anything or not.* Thus, with the best of intentions, the institution creates a situation where the patient's original feeling of worthlessness is confirmed. A camping experience offers the opportunity to create conditions where it does make some difference in terms of life comfort whether the patient does something. The other powerful influence potential in this type of therapy is the use of the small group. The necessity for interaction of a group of a dozen or less can be a far different experience from some mass activity which requires only passive conformity. To me, these are the avenues along which benefits arise.

A welcome addition to this field would be further attempts to quantify what types of camping therapy seem most productive and whether one type of experience will be more useful than another, for some given problem. In contrast with many methods of treatment, camping therapy appears to have many helpful effects, few or no harmful effects, and is usually enjoyed by both the healer and the healed.

THOMAS P. LOWRY, M.D.

ACKNOWLEDGMENTS

PERMISSIONS TO REPUBLISH and quote are gratefully acknowledged as follows:

New Directions Publishing Corporation, for Hesse, Hermann: *Siddhartha,* 1951 edition, p. 138.

U.S. Children's Bureau, for Flax, Norman and Peters, Edward N.: Retarded children at camp with normal children. *Children, 16:*232, 1969.

Dr. Ernest Harms, for Harms, Ernest: Camps as mental health institutions. *Nervous Child, 6:*127, 1947; Redl, Fritz: Psychopathologic risks of camp life. *Children, 6:*139, 1947; Goodrich, Lois: How much decentralized camping can do for the child. *Nervous Child, 6:*202, 1947.

The American Psychiatric Association, for McDonald, Margaret C.: Hospital patients and staff share a wilderness trip in Oregon. *Psychiatr News,* 7 (no. 18, 19 and 20), Sept. 20, Oct. 4 and Oct. 18, 1972; Weisman, Maxwell N.; Mann, Lenora, and Barker, Ben W.: Camping: an approach to releasing human potential in chronic mental patients. *Am J Psychiatry, 123:*166, 1966; Ackerman, Ora K.; Mitsos, Spiro B. and Seymour, A. Margaret: Patients go camping in Indiana. *Ment Hosp, 10:*16, 1959; Smith, Bert K.: Patients go camping in Texas. *Ment Hosp, 10:* 17, 1959; Caplan, Henry K. and Reneau, Robert F.: Young patients enjoy therapeutic camp. *Hosp Community Psychiatry, 16:* 235, 1965; Reitman, E. Edward and Pokorny, Alex D.: A day center goes camping. *Hosp Community Psychiatry, 17:*181, 1966; Caplan, Ruth B.: Tent treatment for the insane. *Hosp Community Psychiatry, 18:*296, 1967; Whittekin, Ruth G.: Imaginative themes enliven day camp. *Hosp Community Psychiatry, 18:*

237, 1967; McFarland, Frances W.; Martin, R. C., and Williams, T. A.: Staff attitudes and patient behavior change on a camping trip. *Hosp Community Psychiatry, 18:*296, 1967; Kole, Delbert M. and Busse, Howard: Trail camping for delinquents. *Hosp Community Psychiatry, 20:*150, 1969; Hobbs, Tom R. and Shelton, George C.: Therapeutic camping for emotionally disturbed adolescents. *Hosp Community Psychiatry, 23:*298, 1972.

CONTENTS

Camping Therapy

CHAPTER I

CAMPING EXPERIENCE AND THE UNCONSCIOUS

JOHN EDWARD TALLEY

MODERN MAN IS AWAKENING to the natural world around him as something more than a source of material wealth.

Hiking, camping and rock climbing provide a means of discovering both the outer natural world and one's inner natural world.

In his lifetime, devoted to studying the complexities of man's nature, Carl Gustav Jung (1874-1961) saw man's task as one of healing the split between nature and reason. There can be no wholeness without honoring this fundamental duality of the psyche.

Jung himself lived his life constantly aware of this. Besides his prodigious intellectual activity and work with patients, he sailed and hiked. He explored primitive wildernesses in his native Switzerland, in the African jungles, in the American Southwest and in the vastness of India and the foothills of the Himalayas. He built himself, stone by stone, beam by beam, a primitive house called Bollingen on the shores of the Lake of Zurich, surrounded by dense forests. There was a well from which he drew water by hand and fireplaces over which he cooked his food and warmed his rooms; light was provided by the sun by day and candles or oil lamps by night. This was his retreat. No electricity, no telephones. Here he watched the animals and the birds and listened to the wind and the running brooks and the lapping of the lake against the shore. And he listened to his own inner nature.

Returning from his explorations of other men's worlds, the world of nature, and his own inner world to his office and home in Zurich, he saw patients, corresponded, taught at the University and at the Burgholzi, and wrote volume upon volume of his discoveries and interpretations of those discoveries.

What is essential to the purpose of this book is Jung's controversial and still today generally misunderstood view of man's psyche as consisting of not only a personal but also a collective or objective unconscious.

The personal unconscious consists of personal experience from the moment of conception (parents, family, peers, community, school, country, world)—that is, all the outer, environmental contributions to his make-up. The collective or objective unconscious consists of his instinctual, natural experience as a member of the species *Homo sapiens.*

The collective unconscious is that stratum of the unconscious which carries the *given* of man, what he comes into the world already possessing. These instincts are more related to the sympathetic than to the central nervous system and probably ultimately to the four fundamental amino acids (thymine, adenine, cytosine and guanine) found in the DNA and RNA of the chromosomes themselves.

Jung saw the collective unconscious as nature itself and that part of us which connects us with the living process.

Man experiences the collective unconscious, i.e., his instincts, in the form of symbols and of affects, which Jung named *archetypal images.*

Whereas an archetype is the instinct itself, physiologic, genetic and ultimately unknowable; the archetypal image is the *manifestation* or intimation of the fundamental instinct in the psyche of man. These archetypal images are expressed in dreams, in myths, in fairy tales, in cosmologies, in religions and, although clothed in the particularities of various individual and cultural experiences, are the base universal for all mankind.

These basic archetypal images can be broadly subsumed under four categories: The Feminine Archetypes, The Masculine Archetypes, The Archetypes of Transformation, and, finally, The Archetypes of Wholeness.

In Jung's cosmology (and every psychology is ultimately the cosmology of the proponent of that school), it is essential that man develop those aspects of his psyche which have been undeveloped. Both ego-consciousness and the collective natural aspects of himself must be in a harmonious relationship.

Jung noted that man historically (as revealed in the manifestations of the collective unconscious) experiences himself originally, just as the infant does, as part of nature; he exists in a state of *participation mystique* with nature.

Through the ages, as an individual develops with the gradual increase of his ego-consciousness, man comes to experience himself as separate from nature, having reached apogee with his present technological *hubris* which regards nature as something to be conquered.

Jung saw that these opposites—the *participation mystique* state and the technological intellectual, ego-centered state—are equally one-sided. (Each is, of course, necessary at a particular stage of development.) Each state, however, leaves man vulnerable to the onslaught of the undeveloped or forgotten opposite. Since man is *both* a creature of nature *and* capable of reasoning (ego-development), neither can be sacrificed permanently without psychological loss to the individual.

Primitive man is totally dependent on external nature. He is at its whim; the nature gods, who are capricious, possess the power of life and death over him and, consequently, require constant propitiation and appeasement. The primitive experiences himself as the *object* of the power of nature.

The conscious, thinking, rational man, proud of (his illusion of) autonomy, is subject to the gods of scientific materialism, whose laws likewise require constant propitiation and appeasement. The rational man experiences himself as the *subject,* i.e. the possessor of power over nature.

Primitive man's task, and that of the developing individual, is to become more conscious and aware of his capacity for understanding and mastering himself and his environment. To survive, he must learn that he can have relatively more choices in determining his life.

And just as important is modern, educated man's task to rediscover and reestablish the long neglected connection between his ego-consciousness and the deep, natural wellsprings of nature within himself, and discover the humbling fact of his own vulnerability and humanity.

The actual physical experience of living in close touch with nature, as one does camping and hiking, provides both the tasks described above. For those undeveloped people still too much identified with nature and lacking ego strength, the experience provides challenge, testing, opportunity for mastery and self-confidence, as well as camaraderie, mutual help and the cooperative spirit—all part of ego development.

(Parenthetically, the psychotic person, living totally in the collective unconscious, at the whim of the terrible gods as was Deborah in *I Never Promised You a Rose Garden,* would benefit in the same way. By experiencing mastery over aspects of external nature, the psychotic would at the same time master the aspects of nature within.)

More obviously, the over-educated, one-sided intellectual, by being thrust into experiencing aspects of his psyche—little used in his technological, specialized day-to-day world—might, with grace, be allowed some sense of the mystery of nature, and hopefully of his own inner microcosm, wherein gods dwell and music plays.

It is not just coincidence that therapy is described over and over again as an inner journey to places and experiences unknown, the therapist along as guide, helper and friend.

Donald Sandner, in a brief and illuminating article on Navajo healing, describes the fundamental steps in the various Navajo healing ritual chants, which last for a number of days and nights. The patient is taken by the Medicine Man on a long symbolic journey going back to the beginnings in a myth of origin, proceeding to the experience of confronting and *identifying* evil, then to the experience of death and finally concluding with rebirth.

When the two *return* to the present, from the journey deep into nature, the ceremony of renewal is performed:

My feet are restored for me.
My legs are restored for me.
My body is restored for me.

My mind is restored for me.
The dust of my feet is restored for me.
My saliva is restored for me.
The hair on my head is restored for me.
The world before me is restored in beauty.
The world behind me is restored in beauty.
The world above me is restored in beauty.
The world below me is restored in beauty.
My voice is restored in beauty.
In beauty it is finished.
In beauty it is finished.
In beauty it is finished.
In beauty it is finished.

REFERENCES

Jung, Carl G.: *Memories, Dreams, Reflections.* New York, Pantheon, 1963.

Osterman, Elizabeth: The tendency toward pattern and order in matter and in the psyche. In Wheelwright, Joseph B. (Ed.): *The Reality of the Psyche.* New York, Putnam, 1968.

Sandner, Donald F.: Healing symbolism in Navajo religion. In *SPRING,* New York, Springer Pub., 1972.

Singer, June: *Boundaries of the Soul.* New York, Doubleday, 1972.

CHAPTER II

EARLY FORMS OF CAMPING IN AMERICAN MENTAL HOSPITALS*

RUTH B. CAPLAN

THE EARLIEST FORM OF CAMPING therapy was instituted by accident. During the first decade of the 20th century, a series of articles appeared in the *American Journal of Insanity* on *tent treatment,* which was purported to be a highly effective method of improving mental and physical health. Patients said to benefit from being cared for in the fresh air included the tubercular, the demented, the filthy, and the convalescent.

Tent treatment is an interesting forerunner of the treatment of psychiatric patients in small groups in a therapeutic environment. Because nobody isolated its basic benefit—personal attention in small groups—this benefit was eventually refined out of existence, although the practice of camping continued for some time.

Tent treatment started as a public health device. In 1901, A. E. Macdonald, M.D., superintendent and medical director of Manhattan State Hospital East on Ward's Island, New York, feared an epidemic of tuberculosis in his overcrowded wards and ordered that isolation tents be erected on the hospital grounds. It was believed that serious mental disorder increased susceptibility to tuberculosis. There was at least one precedent for using tents. In 1884, T. S. Armstrong, M.D., superintendent of the Binghamton (N.Y.) Asylum for the Chronic Insane, had erected tents in order to alleviate gross overcrowding, but it was Dr. Macdonald, nearly twenty years later, who first realized the therapeutic value of tent treatment.

* The first part of this paper appeared as an article, Caplan, Ruth B.: Tent treatment for the insane—an early form of milieu therapy, *Hosp Community Psychiatry, 18*:296, 1967.

On June 5, 1901, he moved forty tubercular patients into two large tents, each with twenty beds. Openings for ventilation were put into the tent walls, and the sides were kept open as much as possible. To insure complete isolation, all working, dining, and sanitary facilities were provided at the camp site. A rich diet was prescribed, and scrupulous cleanliness was maintained.

Camp life was free and interesting. Most of the patients left their beds to wander about the lawn. They watched the steamers and excursion boats passing along the East River, read papers and magazines, played games, and showed increased interest in their surroundings and in their fellow patients.

The results startled and delighted the physicians. The physical and mental improvement of the patients was so marked that another tent was pitched for twenty nontubercular psychiatric patients, sixty percent of whom were bedridden and most of whom were seriously regressed and filthy. This group showed dramatic weight gains, an index of mental health in keeping with the predominantly physiological emphasis of psychiatry of the time. The habits and deportment of the regressed patients also improved, and there was marked decrease in incontinence. Several formerly hopeless patients showed enough improvement to eventually be discharged.

At the end of the summer all but one group of the most seriously ill tubercular patients were returned to the wards. Physicians noted that many regressed to incontinence and withdrawal, while those left in an elaborately winterized tent continued to improve. In the following spring the tent colony was reopened, and general improvement was again seen.

During the following year several detailed and enthusiastic articles discussed tent treatment. The papers were illustrated with photographs of men and women seated on benches and garden chairs near their tents under the trees, with two or three nurses standing behind them. Such photographs were rare in the *American Journal of Insanity* at a time when most plates showed brain dissections or abnormal tissue formations. Apparently nobody realized the role of the small group in the success of tent treatment, although some articles did note the emergence of an *esprit de corps* among campers and an insistence by patients on decorating their tents for visitors. Participating physicians credited improvement to sunlight and *diversity of events.*

Tent treatment became a minor fad in institutions throughout the country, and its course may be traced through the half-yearly summaries of hospital events in the *American Journal of Insanity.* Its popularity was based on several factors: hospitals had to isolate their tuberculosis cases, they were chronically short of space on all wards, and the initial investment in tents was lower than the cost of constructing more solid buildings.

Andrew W. Hoisholt, M.D., of California wrote a number of letters to the editors of the *American Journal of Insanity,* on the aftermath of the 1906 San Francisco earthquake. In one he described the destruction of Agnew Asylum and the fate of its inmates, then housed on the grounds in tents and makeshift lean-tos, many of which the patients had erected themselves.

> "I was astonished to see how nicely the patients got along under the circumstances," he wrote. "Men and women who had been more or less constantly violent and untidy when confined in the building were now getting along peacefully, seldom quarreling, and showing more desire to keep clean than they had done when restricted to the limits of the building and airing courts. They all seemed more comfortable and contented in the tents and on the open grounds. . . . Immediately following the catastrophe . . . many worked like Trojans in the effort to rescue those caught in the wreck and in caring for the wounded. . . . The record of the patients' condition and conduct during the first two or three weeks of this enforced out-door life certainly speaks well for tent treatment. Even the epileptics have had fewer attacks."*

Tent treatment did not retain its prominence for long. It declined because its real value, the small group, was eliminated, while the *superabundance* of fresh air and sunshine was scrupulously maintained. True, some units were made too small, as when one or two beds were placed in revolving tents that could be turned to face the sun, or when pavilions were built to isolate bedridden patients in single rooms. On the other hand, camps were becoming much bigger, housing several hundred patients.

* ——— *Am J Insanity,* 63:131-132, 1906.

In 1903 there were 175 patients in the Ward's Island camps; in 1905 the facilities were to be enlarged to accommodate 300. In most hospitals the problems and expense of heating, maintaining, and frequently replacing the tents led to the erection of wooden pavilions with large windows and sun porches instead of the orthodox canvas tents. The pavilions soon became adjuncts of the wards, overcrowded, locked, understaffed, and underequipped. The whole atmosphere of improvisation, adventure, and group cohesiveness disappeared, as did the concern and pride of the staff and their special attention to individuals in a selected patient population.

In 1910, Binghamton State Hospital announced a new project in the half-yearly summary of the *American Journal of Insanity:*

> A notable feature of the hospital life during the past summer has been the development of a summer camp for convalescent patients on the bank of the Susquehanna River about two miles distant from the main hospital. This camp is located on land owned by the hospital and consists of several small buildings in rustic design and a number of tents. It accommodates thirty patients and the employees necessary for their care. A daily wagon service conveys supplies to the camp and a telephone enables the nurse in charge to communicate at once with the medical office. Besides the patients regularly quartered at the camp, who remain as a rule a fortnight, daily visits are made by many who are not well enough to warrant their remaining continuously at the camp, and these outings have been found highly beneficial. Boating, fishing, bathing, croquet, etc., are enjoyed by some of these patients, while others have found the music of the gramophone or books in a small library entertaining. The camp life is regarded as a valuable part of the treatment of the recovered patients.*

For the next ten years, Binghamton regularly sent news of "Pine Camp," as it came to be called, to the *Journal.* In 1912, the facilities were made more permanent. *Rustic frame structures with canvas sides* replaced the dormitory and dining room tents in order to withstand storms and cold weather. And besides housing convalescent patients for stays of two to three weeks, the

---

* *Am J Insanity,* 445,1910-11.

camp was also opened to other patients, six of whom were dispatched daily for a few hours on the river bank, and returned to the wards at night.

In 1913, the hospital announced that,

> Nearly all to whom this privilege has been extended have enjoyed the outing and in almost every instance striking benefit has been noted, especially as regards gain in weight, the increase ranging from one or two to ten or eleven pounds after a fortnight's stay.*

By 1915, the focus of Pine Camp had changed from serving convalescent cases to providing a therapeutic experience for the acutely ill, "It is believed that a considerable number of patients start on the road to recovery while sojourning at the camp."

Unlike Tent Treatment, this form of camping never spread widely. A few institutions arranged outings for patients on boats, and in 1916, Bloomingdale Hospital announced that for several years, it had owned a beach cottage to which patients were brought for day trips, though a few stayed longer. A recovered patient was quoted as saying, "The Beach Cottage part of the summer of 1915 was the beginning of my improvement and we all felt that it was the lift we otherwise would not have had.†

Although Binghamton continued to send news of Pine Camp to the *Journal*, the tone of the notices grew dull and stereotyped. The same points were listed each year, as though all excitement and inventiveness had drained out of the project. And, unlike Tent Treatment, no full length articles appeared on the benefits of this treatment scheme. In 1920, the news stopped. The *American Journal of Insanity* became the *American Journal of Psychiatry*, and the gossipy half-yearly summaries vanished, with their tales of political intrigues in asylum management, murderous assaults by patients, the installation of electric plants and parking lots, the adoption of new treatment schemes, the management of cholera epidemics among the hospital's hogs or tuberculosis in the cows, etc. Thus, camping slipped out of sight until it was rediscovered in the late 1950's and early 1960's.

*——— *Am J Insanity,* :417, 1915-1916.

† *Am J Insanity,* 333-334, 1916-1917.

CHAPTER III

CAMPING THERAPY IN THE COMMONWEALTH OF MASSACHUSETTS

Elizabeth Mary Remar and Thomas P. Lowry

Camping in the modern day Massachusetts mental hospital system had its Renaissance at Monson State Hospital, a facility for epileptics, which began a camping program in 1961, with a program that continues today as a day camp for all patients.

In 1966, Dr. Milton Greenblatt, now Commissioner of Mental Health, instituted a camping program at Boston State Hospital. Thirty-seven patient campers traveled to Camp Denison on the shores of Lake Balpate in rural Massachusetts. Since funds were short, the staff was almost entirely volunteer: housewives, college and high school students and even two Vista volunteers. The patients were of all ages and diagnoses, with lengths of hospitalization from months to years. There was no clear idea which patients would benefit most, so it was decided to send a mixed batch of rather chronic patients for eight nights. The first outing was successful, and in 1967 was repeated with sixty patients, again keeping the cost low by using donated camp facilities in the off season. Comments were solicited from the patients at the end of camp. A selection will convey how most of them felt.

> I had a good time at camp. The shows and swimming really made me happy. We had a nice time in the dining room. It was friendly and like home. I made new friends and the food was excellent. I hope we can make it again, because it is something people should do—make new friends and be happy. Mary M.
>
> I liked the idea of camp because of the courtesy of all the patients and the manner that they conducted themselves, because of the little week's vacation away from steady work at the hospital. Norma M.
>
> For the first time in my life. I have laughed; I have God. Elspeth S.

Certainly the tenor of these notes indicates a pleasure in living and making friends, both scarce commodities in a long-term hospital population. Prolonged stay in a large hospital, combined with the patient's previous difficulties in interpersonal gratification, tend to promote a passive deterioration in many patients. The camp experience seemed to bring out the best in patients and to allow opportunity for further growth and development. The success of the program led to its continuation; in 1972, camping at Boston State Hospital was eliminated because of inadequate funds.

Massachusetts has sixteen state facilities, including psychiatric hospitals, schools for the retarded and a regional mental health center. As of the summer of 1972, ten of these facilities had active summer camping programs and six did not, usually because of no money.

The overall experiences of these various programs has suggested several general principles which might be useful to others, who are planning camping programs. The first observation is that three different types of programs should be created: one for disturbed adolescents (who require large muscle activity and close supervision); one for the chronic patients who need strong remotivation efforts to rouse them from their withdrawal and torpor; and finally, one for less disturbed patients already in a day care or rehabilitation sheltered workshop program. For these latter patients, many of whom have made a satisfactory place in life in a hospital job, the camp may be a week's vacation from their fulltime work.

Staff ratios of three patients to one staff member are satisfactory for most groups; for adolescents, a one to one ratio is far more desirable. Patients should also be grouped by age. The very elderly, of course, move more slowly, but the normal adult patient, after years of indolence and medication will also tire relatively easily. The staff found that medication frequently needed review and often reduction or elimination in the camp environment.

Four groups of patients should be excluded from the camp programs: the non-ambulatory; the brittle diabetic; the patient in delirium tremens; the addict in active withdrawal. Patient-campers are already complex enough; these additional factors make camp life almost impossible, without special and expensive facilities.

Often the camping experience is as much an awakening for the staff as for the patients. Staff tend to lean upon their positions of authority. (Big Daddy knows best; I have keys and you don't; if you're not crazy, what are you doing here?) Especially with the many volunteers present, the atmosphere is much more one of camper and counselor or even just two campers. With this shift in status, the patient is both obliged to and able to exhibit sane behavior, while the staff person expects less crazy behavior, thus breaking the chain of self-fulfilling prophecies that characterize many hospital interactions.

The use of volunteers was originally based on fiscal reasons: volunteers were free. Even if funds were unlimited, volunteers have something special to offer and should be kept. The fact that they aren't doing it for money produces great emotional leverage with some patients. The fact that volunteers are relatively innocent and enthusiastic is another factor which makes them specially valuable.

The ordinary crises of camp life should be handled as much as possible through patient initiative. Patients are told that if they wish to change cabins or groups, it is up to them to initiate the request. Other suggestions and requests are also encouraged.

In summary, camping therapy has offered many benefits. It can be done with most types of patients, in a wide variety of settings. If more funds were available, even more should be done.

CHAPTER IV

ADVENTURE CAMPING AT OREGON STATE HOSPITAL*

MARGARET C. McDONALD

INTRODUCTION

WHAT HAPPENS when fifty-one chronic mental patients and fifty-one hospital staff members take a two-week wilderness camping trip? Well—what happened was that almost everyone had a "damn good time," learned something about himself and how he relates to others outside a defined setting, and had stories of mountains conquered, rivers run, and personal reflections made to tell those who stayed behind at the hospital. And most of what happened on the mountain was what Dr. Dean Brooks, superintendent of Oregon State Hospital, and Luther Jerstad, Everest conqueror and president of Lute Jerstad Adventures, had anticipated, hoped for, and arranged during the previous year.

On July 30, buses arrived at Anthony Lakes, Oregon, bringing fifty-one people from the patient ranks and fifty-one staff members from all wards of Oregon State Hospital—people who would come together as equals during the two-week adventure camp that had taken a full year to plan and execute.

Most of the patients had been in the hospital more than six months, and many had been there from ten to twenty years. Most were schizophrenic, some had character disorders, a few had raped and/or murdered, and a fair number had used drugs; none were "easy" cases. But Dr. Brooks feels that patients often remain chronically ill, not because of their mental problems, but because relatives, friends, hospital staff, and they themselves tend

* The October 27, 1972 LIFE magazine has a photo essay which also describes the Oregon program.

to stereotype them into a dependency-illness role, ignoring latent strengths and capacities for growth. "They may," says Dr. Brooks, "literally be drained of self-confidence and respect through the dehumanization and depersonalization that inevitably creep into every social institution."

Dr. Brooks had observed the individual and group changes occurring in a group of Girl Scouts who went on a two-week mountaineering expedition, and he became convinced that a similar experience could help his patients and staff establish mutual trust and interdependency. He hoped his group would be able to find new potentials as they met the challenges of a natural environment in which patients and staff members alike would be compelled to alter roles in order to fare well. Personalities would come down to the more basic and universal characteristics of human nature—at least, this is what he hoped.

Lute Jerstad and his professional guide staff led the camp, which was held in three parts—white water boating, rock climbing, and survival ecology. The large group of 102 was divided into three smaller groups for the actual adventures, and each group alternated activities, returning to base camp after every four days for one day of rest in which new equipment would be picked up and supplies put in order for the next phase of the camp.

Everything that happened was documented on film, a key in plans for follow-up therapy, in which a patient will be able to relive his successful challenges by viewing them again. "This reinforcement of his achievement should keep alive the desire to enter a world full of unknown rather than to revert to the known, controlled world of institution life."

Oregon State Hospital Adventure Camp was born a year ago when Dr. Brooks and Lute Jerstad first began discussing the feasibility of such an outing. Of course, a major problem was funding. But Dr. Brooks knows how to *operate,* and, with a great many telephone calls and explanations, the money slowly began coming in. Major contributors included the Truman Wesley Collins Foundation, the Bullitt Foundation, the Edwards Foundation, Hall Pendleton, the Millicent Foundation, Georgia Pacific, and the Oregon State Hospital staff.

And those who couldn't offer money offered goods or services. Radium Hot Springs pool in Baker, Oregon, was opened for the hospital crew any time they wanted to swim. Larmer Transfer brought in over two tons of supplies, the National Guard let the group borrow tents, Cutter and Dome Laboratories contributed insect repellent and sunscreen, and the people of the Baker community gave a steak fry and rodeo in honor of all participants.

Plans were so tentative that up until two weeks prior to the beginning of the camp, Dr. Brooks was not sure that enough funds would be raised to put his plans into action.

But everyone knew that the word was go when supplies began arriving, members of the press were invited to participate, and patients began wearing their boots around the hospital.

The trip was a sure success when the buses arrived at Anthony Lakes and the first patient stepped off grinning from ear to ear.

THE CAMP BEGINS

When my plane landed in Pendleton, Oregon, I was still wondering what he would look like, but Dr. Dean Brooks and I immediately recognized each other. In five minutes we were in the car with another newly-arrived observer headed toward Anthony Lakes, the base camp site for the first Oregon State Hospital Adventure Camp. We had barely pulled out onto the highway when Dr. Brooks began—

> "I'd like this camp to be an exercise in absolute trust. Our patients will range in age from sixteen to sixty; there will be schizophrenics, sex offenders, narcotics addicts—everything. We haven't picked the easy cases. Patients, like staff members, will keep a log. Our participants were chosen on the basis of interest, after seeing a film of the Girl Scouts and hearing Lute Jerstad lecture—they thought Lute was the most wonderful man they had ever seen. Most of them have been in the hospital at least six months. That was one of the criteria. I tried to choose people who had been hospitalized for a long time."

And so the discussion went, with Dr. Brooks ("Call me Dean") enthusiastically answering endless questions. The following day, support staff would arrive. Most of the supplies, more than two tons I was told, were already at base camp waiting to be distributed.

Support staff did indeed arrive the following day, along with most of Lute Jerstad's staff of guides, who would be sharing their outdoor knowledge with us during the two weeks to come. The guides would not be told which campers were patients and which were staff—people would be people. However, each patient had already been assigned a staff one-to-one, to be with him almost twenty-four hours a day for the next two weeks. And not all staff members were from the professional ranks of the hospital; there were student nurses, painters, maintenance personnel, recreational therapists, and even a TV repairman. Sometimes patient and staff member were deliberately paired; sometimes the choice was random. In some cases partners were the same sex; in some, opposite sexes were paired.

Late the following afternoon, the participants arrived, two busloads full, with an overflow in assorted cars and vans—all excited, many obviously quite sick—a woman who looked as though she were pregnant but was not, a man with one eye, an Indian girl with forearms covered with scars. Dr. Brooks greeted the group, gear was distributed with some confusion, tents were assigned, and a few small crises were taken care of. Tomorrow things would really begin.

Everyone was up at least an hour before breakfast; and breakfast was at 6:30. First major job of the day was a section meeting. The 102 campers had been divided into three groups in order to alternately participate in three activities—river running, rock climbing, and survival ecology. Each section of the adventure would take four days, followed by a rest day. I would accompany Group B, which would do survival ecology first. We met with our head guide for the trip, Scotty Steeves, a twin for Santa Claus with three dogs mimicking his gait as they followed him. The campers fell in love with Scotty, who gave us a brief explanation of what we would be doing in the woods and what we should bring in our packs.

There was swimming in the afternoon at Radium Hot Springs pool, donated free of charge to all campers during the entire two weeks. We enjoyed the warm water, the diving boards, basketball, and especially the slides. Sarah, a schizophrenic patient who was to be in my group, said, "I was really scared, so I went down the little one first. It was fun." A girl who had refused to come out of her tent the night before was willing to come to the pool, although she did not want to swim.

When we came back to camp from swimming, sick bay had been set up in the bar of the lodge. "What kind of shots do they give in there?" asked Jerry, known as the "Prolixin Kid."

Camp was officially underway, though, when we left for the woods the next morning with Scotty and his dog Smoky in the lead. Our packs had been loaded with clothes and personal items, tarps for shelter, cans for cooking, and some provisions. Hiking was hard with forty pounds of gear, but everyone managed. Jackie, a 15-year-old patient, 4 ft and 7 in tall, threw her pack down about 200 feet into the trail and vehemently declared that she wouldn't come—but she came, and most of the time she carried her pack.

We found our first wild food beside the path during a rest stop; tart, delicious huckleberries. Sarah, after trying the slide at the pool, tried sliding down a hill (accidentally) and didn't like it. But she wasn't hurt and the group agreed that she did look funny. Sarah fared well, although she fell many more times during the day.

Further up the trail Scotty showed us some wild lady fern and taught us how to gather it to add to our stew; we also gathered strawberry leaves for tea. Around three in the afternoon we made camp, divided into small groups, learned how to make shelters with our tarps, and prepared dinner.

After dinner Jackie, along with Donna, an 18-year-old American Indian patient, came over to talk to me; they discussed their hospital, drug, sex, and runaway experiences.

As dark came on, many of us exchanged backrubs and gratefully went to sleep.

The second day, we hiked only three miles to a lovely meadow; we were tired from yesterday's hike, many were slow, and two got sick. Shelters the second night were much more elaborate than the first. Campers had learned new ways to put up tarps and were even adding rain ponchos in order to make four-walled shelters. During the afternoon there was time for fishing and gathering wild onions for seasoning. Donna caught three fish and ate them in the Indian tradition—raw. But there were problems among the good times.

A guide had heard Donna and Jackie talking about being scared and asked them what they were scared of. Jackie told him that Donna was depressed, had found an old piece of tin, and was thinking about cutting herself. He talked to Donna, but she described herself as a *brick wall* who listened but did not hear. Nevertheless, she was persuaded to talk to our physician Ben Wight. Donna had been sick on the trail, had arrived in camp later than her one-to-one, a student nurse who was now out fishing, and now she was depressed and did not like herself.

Ben got the piece of tin from her and got her to go to bed, but she got up during the night and slashed herself with a piece of glass she had found. Her depression touched us all. There were a few other signs of problems in camp, but things in general were still going well. Jackie for the first time showed some interest in what the rest of her group was doing and offered to help them. Two more days to go.

We climbed a steep hill the third day to be rewarded by a lovely small lake as our campsite. Donna cut herself again on the trail; her problems seemed more acute than anyone else's. She had been returned to her small group of four and they were to be responsible for handling her problem among themselves. Most group problems seemed to arise when one-to-ones did not stay with each other, especially on the trail. One small group almost left camp before everyone this morning, leaving one of the patients belonging to their group in camp without even knowing where they were. Fortunately, they were caught before starting on the trail, but the patient who was left asked for a new partner.

On the last day, declared Ben and Scotty, no one would be allowed to walk faster than the slowest person in the group. If one person had to stop, all would stop. Those working well together were having a great trip, but those who were having trouble with their partners were more than ready for the four days to be over.

On our last day, we had a tremendous amount of energy. We

were eager for a good meal, although our rice, sardine, and wild onion stews weren't too bad. We stopped a mile above base camp to look down into the valley and to eat the remainder of our trail fare. And though the last mile to camp was the longest of the trip, feet would not stop walking. Scotty gave each of us a bear hug and said goodbye as we arrived, and one of our patients began to cry. When asked why there were tears in her eyes, she said, "I don't know." Another patient, Sarah, when asked how she did, answered, "It's the best I've ever done."

We were all tired, hungry, and dirty, but somehow, once we were back in camp, we remembered the warmth of campfires, the wild mountain sage, and the new experiences, rather than the blisters, mosquito bites, and periods of depression. We had formed a cohesion that would stay with the group on the river and on the rocks.

ON THE RIVER RAFTS

We rose early the day Group B was to leave for the river, for it would take us three hours by bus to reach the site where we would *put in;* that is, launch our bright yellow rubber rafts in the Grand Ronde River. Our doctor, Ben Wight, set the mood for the day when he came to breakfast whistling the Beatles' "Yellow Submarine."

When we arrived, the guides had the boats ready for us to pack with our personal gear, which we had stored the night before in rubber bags. We blew up small pillows to place in the bottom of the rafts, were issued life jackets, and were given some instructions about rowing and about what to do should we tip over.

There were more changes than just the terrain we were exploring in moving from forest to river, mainly that each of us could be in a boat with whomever we chose. Before we started down the river, our head guide, Rob Cooley, instructed us to travel with anyone we wished except our *one-to-ones.* (Each patient was normally paired with a staff member.) He said, "You see them enough, so go with someone else, and change partners whenever you want to." This set the pace for the casualness that was to pervade the river trip and that provided a welcome relief from the tension we had begun to experience toward the end of our survival trip.

For the first leg of the journey, I went with Ben, our doctor, and Jim, a teen-age patient. I had noticed during the survival trip that Jim was often sleepy, usually sitting with his head hanging and his eyes closed. He never spoke unless asked a direct question; yet when he did respond he seemed to comprehend well and to have a good attention span. When Ben and I discussed Jim's behavior with his staff partner, she said he was on too much medication to stay awake. Ben reduced the medication, and soon we were on our way down the Grand Ronde River.

Rowing wasn't nearly as easy as the guides had made it sound, and for a while there were yellow boats everywhere except where they should be. It was really hard—we could push or pull with the oars, we could row with one oar or two—but whatever we did, the boat went exactly the way we didn't want it to go. One boat was punctured five minutes after being launched.

But soon we began to understand the logistics of rowing a boat and, more important, we mastered the technique of water fighting. Water fights served two purposes: first, they were fun, and second, they cooled us off, for the temperature on the river exceeded 100 degrees.

Jim, when asked, consented to row our raft for a while. He had some difficulty learning the rowing techniques and didn't seem to enjoy himself too much, but he did stay with it for about a half hour or so.

As campers realized that a third of their adventure was over and they were already on the second leg, and having fun doing it, some changes in attitude began to show. Patients seemed to gain self confidence, and many staff members were quite bewildered at not being needed. In some cases, the new attitudes brought confusion. One patient, caught in the flux of decision, still signaled through some of her actions that she needed to be taken care of, and when a staff member responded to the signals, she complained about being treated like a child.

Another patient, Harold, had observed on the trail that his staff partner was impatient. The staffer, Lou, countered that Harold was unresponsive. But when we changed partners on the river, Lou showed impatience with several other people too, even to the point of jumping out of a boat when a girl didn't catch on to rowing immediately.

We made our way down the river until late afternoon when we made camp at a beach on the river bank. Guides, patients, and staff members all worked together to prepare a delicious spaghetti supper, supervised by our cook, Claire—a welcome treat after the sardine soup of the survival trip. Soon after our meal, we all crawled into our sleeping bags for the night.

I awoke shortly after I went to sleep when I heard a girl cry, "No, I can't go over there. There's a baby buried over there." Jackie, our smallest and youngest patient, was having vivid agitating hallucinations. She had awakened Dr. Bob Jones, our psychologist and official observer, who was trying unsuccessfully to calm her. Soon several more campers who were sleeping nearby were also awakened, and no one slept until about 5:30 A.M., when Ben gave Jackie a tranquilizing injection simply because she was completely exhausted.

We salvaged an hour or two of sleep, but too soon we were up for breakfast and on the river. Jackie slept in the supply boat all day, but the rest of us weren't so lucky—the rafts had to be rowed, and we were needed to help. Ben stayed with Jackie, so I was by myself with Jim in our boat. He was more awake and responsive than on the first day. He asked to row, and often became frustrated, but even his cursing was good to hear. After some rather tricky rapids, he became upset and asked me to take over, but later he was willing to try again and was really getting the hang of it.

We soon learned, however, that Jim did not like water fights. When we stopped for lunch, the inevitable water fight started, and Jim was doused by our head guide, Rob. He became furious, yelled at us, and walked down the bank to be alone. No one else threw water on him.

Our second night in camp, we shared songs around a campfire, a traditional activity, filled with warm feelings. The night passed uneventfully, with Jackie sleeping all the way through.

Our third day on the river was perhaps the most pleasant. We had learned to row and could relax a bit and enjoy the scenery, which included an eagle soaring above the treetops. Jim really seemed alive, showed some interest in swimming, and just smiled when Bob told him that water fights were part of the trip too.

Our third night's camp was at an old homestead with an orchard by the riverside—and rattlesnakes. We ate dinner, including fresh apple cobbler with fruit from the orchard, and we were just taking a short walk when the first snake was found. After some screaming, it was thrown into the river to swim down river, but many campers became especially cautious. All through the night, we saw sleeping bags walking around in search of a more snakeless place to sleep. One rattler about three feet long was killed by several campers, but we were assured by Rob that the nasty beasties usually stay away from people. Nevertheless, many slept by the fire, which remained well stoked.

Our last morning on the river, we feasted on french toast, bacon, and rattlesnake steak. We launched our boats with the uneasy feeling that this was our last three hours on the river. Water fights were the big thing; Ellie soaked Ben almost before he could crawl out of his sleeping bag. Jim got a bucketful of water in the face and not only laughed about it but retaliated, hitting his enemy right between the eyes. Although he still hung his head a lot, when he looked up there was a sparkle in his eye and a slight smile on his lips. The river seemed to have been good for him.

We took out our boats at a bridge as planned, and the buses were there to meet us with sandwiches and cold drinks. We all seemed to share the opinion that the ride back to camp was far too long and the run down the river far too short.

AT A RANCH RODEO

The folks of the Baker, Oregon, community spread their arms wide open in welcoming the 102 campers from Oregon State Hospital with a steak fry and rodeo at one of the largest ranches in the area. Although the event served its public relations purposes, with campers meeting some of the contributors who made the camp possible, there was a casual down-home atmosphere that put everyone, campers and guests alike, at friendly ease.

We were first greeted by a local group of square dancers who entertained us with a few of their routines. But when guides, campers, and just about everyone else decided to get into the act, the leader's calls of "do-si-do" and "swing your partner" weren't executed nearly as smoothly, and the dance ended with everyone rolling with laughter on the grass.

Twangs of good ole country music filled the air as we relaxed on the lawn enjoying the fine fiddle playing and guitar picking of the band invited to play for us. But when they started playing "Red River Valley," they were joined by a harmonica we hadn't heard before. It was the harmonica of Ray, who shared his heart with us in the traditional melody. Ray, a patient, had lost his eye by heeding the Biblical advice, "If thy right eye offend thee, pluck it out." His simple, honest attitude was not distorted as his notes came through the microphone to touch the souls of all who heard.

Soon Ray was joined by Gloria, another patient, who lives with the fantasy that she is going to bear a child. Gloria joined in singing "On Top of Old Smoky" in a soft, clear soprano that made us feel like she really had lost a lover, maybe on the mountain we were sharing together. Soon, the microphone was surrounded by patients, staffers, and even a journalist singing a medley of country music—"Your Cheating Heart," "Down in the Valley," and many other favorites.

The focus turned to food as we stuffed ourselves with steak so tender it could be cut with a plastic knife, corn on the cob, crisp green salad, and piping hot griddle bread, all prepared with loving hands by women from the community. Scotty, a trail guide, got quite a doggie bag for his canine friends that night.

Those of us who could still move after the feast wandered over to the corral to watch the rodeo, where we saw some local cowboys going through their paces with quarter horses and riding bulls like they were just old milk cows—it did look easy, so easy that some campers decided to try. One of our staff members, Steve, took a rather bad fall from a Brahma bull and had to be taken to lie down. His patient partner was right on Dr. Brooks' heels, saying, "Don't be upset, I'll take care of him, he'll be all right, I'll take care of him. . . ." And he did, too.

Around nine in the evening, dark came on, and we were all full of food, music, and fun. It was time to head back to camp. As soon as we returned, many campers began writing frantically in their diaries before they forgot all they wanted to tell about the rodeo, but Jerry, the "Prolixin Kid," just said, "I'm having too much fun to write in mine."

MOUNTAIN CLIMBING

Camp was well into its second week, and Group B, having completed its adventures on the river and in the forest, had but one more foe to face, the rocks. We had heard from the groups before us of the challenge the rocks offered and of the feeling of accomplishment they got at having faced and conquered them. Near-miracles had already taken place on the rocks. Father Callan, the hospital's lame priest, had rappelled down the 80-foot practice cliff with cane in hand, and Jerry's nickname had been changed from "Prolixin Kid" to "Mountain Goat" because of his skill and daring.

The site for rock climbing was only a mile away from base camp, so the group working on the rocks stayed in camp for the adventure, hiking to the practice site every morning.

The hike to the cliff was almost as hard as trying to climb the rocks themselves, and on the first morning some of us were sure we'd never get there. But Ross, one of our guides, set what he called "an old man's pace" that all of us appreciated and were able to keep up with.

When we arrived, our head guide, Del, began to explain what we would be learning during the next few days. Our first exercise would be bouldering, that is, walking across the face of a rock, in our case no higher than we would like to fall. Del began to explain how to do it: "This is a foothold. You may not be able to see it, but it's there and it will hold you." Well, the foothold was so narrow we really couldn't see it. Then Del stepped on what looked like nothing, and began his climb up the rock. "In order for this foothold to work," he continued, "you must put your weight directly above it. Don't lean in toward Mother Earth, because that won't help you. Keep your weight directly above your hold." He demonstrated again, this time brushing the dust off his invisible foothold before stepping onto it in a ballet-like move.

It looked nearly impossible, but most of us proceeded anyway, starting across the face of the cliff following the easy holds at first, but soon finding ourselves using some that weren't much bigger than the ones Del had pointed out to us. It was frightening in a strangely exhilarating way that compelled us to continue even though our knees were trembling.

After some practice bouldering, we were taught our next step toward conquering the cliff, tying the knots that would keep us attached to our ropes, literally our life lines. We were first given flat pieces of webbing called *swami belts,* which we learned to wrap around our waists very tightly several times and tie in a flat *water knot.* To this belt the all-important rope would be fastened with a *figure eight knot,* and we would be ready to go on to the next step, *belaying,* a procedure using ropes and metal spikes to support one climber's holding safety for someone else as he climbs.

To make sure belayer and climber know what each is doing, specific signals are used. First the climber questions the belayer, "On belay?" to which the belayer answers, "Belay on." The climber says, "Climbing," the belayer, checking his rope again, replies, "Climb," and the ascent begins. All afternoon we practiced climbing and belaying, even making test falls in each position so that we would know how it felt to fall and be caught or to catch someone who is falling. As we left the mountain in the afternoon, we were looking forward to returning the next day.

On the second day of rocks, many people didn't want to hike up to the practice site. Several were actually sick, and most of the others seemed to be just tired—after all we were nearing the end of two solid weeks of very strenuous activity. Peggy, a patient, expressed the feeling of fatigue very well, "I'm tired. If I walked up that mountain I wouldn't do anything. I want to rest today. Besides, don't I have any voice in this camp? Don't I have the right to make a decision about what I want to do for one single day?" Peggy stayed in camp.

Nevertheless, most of us went back up for a second try. We limbered up by practicing bouldering, then spent most of the day learning to *rappel.* Rappelling is a method of letting yourself down a cliff on a rope. Del taught us how to make a diaper seat and to hook up a braking system of carabiners on the rope so that we could make a slow descent. We practiced at various stations set up along the cliff face, the highest being about halfway up. We worked individually until time to head back to camp. Tomorrow would really be the last day to practice our newly acquired skills, because the fourth day would be spent climbing two nearby peaks.

The third day started off well when several people who stayed in camp the day before, including Peggy, were ready to go when we started up the trail on the third morning. The air was full of excitement as people talked about trying to make more difficult climbs on this final day. A major surprise came when Peggy immediately upon reaching the practice site tied herself into a swami and rope, found a belayer, and proceeded to climb the entire face of the cliff and rappel the full eighty feet down. As she reached the bottom, she said, "Well, I've done my work for the day." And the surprises continued–Joe climbed, Roger climbed, Lou climbed, so many people climbed that at one point as many of us were on top of the cliff as were watching down below. There were waiting lines at all rappel stations. Sarah, who had been a real trooper all through camp, taking falls and getting up only to continue each time without complaining, made a climb and rappel of about twenty-five feet, remarking, "To me this was as high as that whole mountain, and I feel good about it."

But one of our real miracles on the last day was Susie's climb. The first day, Susie had complained about the steepness of the trail up to our site. She had whined, acted childish, and asked to go back to the hospital. But she was encouraged by a patient guide to try climbing. First she was three feet up, then four, then walking across the face. The next day she learned to do short rappels and made some higher climbs. And on the third day she was one of a very few female patients who wanted to try the big cliff.

She was frightened as she tied in to start her climb. She took a deep breath and began the series of signals to her belayer, "On belay?" And slowly up the cliff she went. She went carefully, her knees visibly trembling. But she continued up and further up. And then she fell. But she was quickly caught by her belayer who held her with ease for the few seconds it took to find a hold. Now Susie was shaking, she was crying, she called out, "I'm scared." But she kept going up. And she reached the top.

Now she had to come down. She was frightened as she looked back down over the cliff. But she assembled her carabiner braking system and prepared to rappel. Del would rappel beside her to give her confidence.

The two of them started the descent. The first step over the top is the hardest. As Susie came closer to the bottom, she became easier with the rope, going a little faster, moving from side to side. As she touched ground and began unhooking, she said to those around her, "If I can do this, I can solve my own problems, can't I?"

Our final day of adventure camp was an appropriate end to our two-week experience, for we climbed Lookout Peak and its sister Angel Peak (elevation over 8,000 feet) and looked down on all the country we had walked through in the two weeks before. Thoughts were deep as we came down from the peak. Many patients were verbalizing "what I'm going to do when I get out of the hospital." Some talked about jobs, some about husbands and boyfriends; but almost all had definite ideas now, whereas they had seen their futures only in the hospital at the camp's beginning. Jim, who had begun to open up on the river, was now starting conversations with others. Donna was talking about facing her fears by writing them into poems instead of cutting them into her arms. Sarah and Susie had new-found confidence; we all had memories.

As we came down the trail on that last day into camp, the people who had been on survival were also coming in, and soon the buses came back from the river. We were all together again, and after dinner Dr. Brooks expressed his thanks to all who had participated. One camper suggested the formation of a club for the charter members of the first Oregon State Hospital Adventure Camp, and a staff member enthusiastically told the group about watching his partner gain self-reliance. Father Callan summed up the camp in the phrase, "I dare because you care."

The buses and cars left the next morning to return to the hospital. Guides left to return to college. Journalists returned to their bureaus. We all went back to our *normal lives,* but none of us really left the mountain.

CHAPTER V

STAFF ATTITUDE CHANGE IN CAMPING THERAPY WITH CHRONIC PATIENTS

Frances W. McFarland, Robert C. Martin, and Theodore A. Williams

Patients hospitalized for more than a year who either have gotten *lost* in their present work assignments or have been unable to handle any work assignment at all are the major burden and the most neglected in state institutions. The hospital improvement project at Stockton State Hospital, begun in July 1964, deals with the familiar problem of providing effective treatment for such patients.

The goals of the project, which is supported by the National Institute of Mental Health, are to intensify treatment by applying techniques of group therapy and small-group interaction on the job, and to achieve better coordination of industrial therapy with the over-all hospital treatment program. Eleven groups of ten patients each work under the direction and support of group leaders. Most of the leaders are psychiatric technicians, but some are hospital laundry workers who have been receiving special training in working with patients. The leaders are considered participant-observers rather than straw bosses. In the project we emphasize the development of interpersonal relationships and increased responsibility and initiative on the job.

Of the 188 patients who took part in the project in the first two years, almost fifteen percent have been hospitalized sixteen to twenty years, and about thirty percent have been hospitalized twenty-one or more years. Their median age is forty-eight, but a fourth of them are fifty-five or older. About two-thirds of the patients are women. Seventy-five percent of them are diagnosed as being schizophrenic, and twenty-five percent as having chronic brain syndromes.

Although psychiatric ratings by physicians and behavior ratings by ward staff and group leaders show that the patients in the project make significant progress, the progress is very slow. These patients have long demonstrated their ability to insulate themselves and have managed to remain unaffected by a variety of treatment approaches. The work situation apparently does have some advantage in externalizing their problems; it further requires that the patients establish at least embryonic human relationships embodying communication and cooperation. The degree of success we have had in modifying their well-established, rigid defenses does not alleviate their social problems, which are partly a result of long hospitalization. The patients appear to be disengaged from the world, with very little in the way of ties to family or friends, and they have to deal with the added problems of aging in our society.

We originally believed that those who developed work habits and skills could be vocationally rehabilitated. But we soon found that this was not a realizable goal for most project members. However, the increased possibility of placing discharged patients in semi-supervised living situations encouraged us to redefine our treatment goals to include the required social adjustment.

By the end of the first year, we realized that resocialization and remotivation techniques should be added to the program. The work situation was therefore limited to a minimum of twenty hours and maximum of thirty hours a week, with added emphasis on involving small groups in off-duty recreational activities. Hospital facilities and funds were used for picnics, a Friday afternoon social hour, and attendance at athletic events and theater parties. But we felt that the patients should receive some tangible reward, in the form of a more elaborate off-grounds activity for accomplishing significant work. A camping trip was conceived from the wish "Wouldn't it be nice if we could . . ."; the first one took place in August 1966.

From the beginning, patients were involved in discussing and planning for the five-day excursion. They were aware of the problems of locating a suitable camp site and knew that the project budget made no provision for such activities. The lack of money in this case turned into an advantage. The possibilities for fund-raising were discussed in small groups, and it was decided to sponsor a pancake brunch for hospital staff and patients. The groups laid out a campaign for selling tickets and participated actively. They handled the money, prepared the food, and served the brunch to approximately 600 patients and staff members. The patients' enthusiasm, actually more like mere cracks in the wall of apathy that usually surrounded them, seemed to be contagious, even outside the project. Not only did the project patients feel that they were making a real contribution toward the trip, but other patients and staff shared in the excitement.

The brunch was a general morale booster, an innovation that received widespread approval and support. It was also, incidentally, a big social event for some of the geriatric patients, who enjoyed "going out to eat." The net proceeds were about 350 dollars, which was almost enough to meet the camp-site bill of 375 dollars. The staff-patient committee in charge of the patient benefit fund agreed to pay for the cost of transportation and provide a fresh-milk fund.

One ward responded to those activities by donating a patchwork quilt, which had been made on the ward, for a raffle. Again the groups worked at selling tickets, and they netted another 150 dollars, putting the trip in the black. In retrospect, the fund-raising was a crucial part of the trip. It made the excursion directly the product of the patients' efforts, even with the considerable support and direction of the group leaders.

The food service arranged for most of the food and was generous both in the supplies furnished and in the time given to set up menus and instruct the three group leaders who comprised the food committee. Menu planning and requests for some special foods came out of the group discussions also. The groups working at gardening were able to fill in with their fresh fruit and vegetables. The extra money that had been raised made it possible to buy ice, potato chips, and snacks that the hospital could not provide.

The committee structure was generally adopted as the easiest way to handle other operations, such as camp housekeeping, recreation, and clothing. Groups constituted committees *in toto*, with the group leader acting as liaison with departments when necessary. The groups who worked in the laundry had an inside track on bedding, linens, and extra clothes and managed adequate supplies. The groups received full cooperation with the camping project from all sources, especially the food service, the business services, the ward staffs, and the rehabilitation services. The actual camping staff consisted of nine group leaders (two men and seven women) and two registered nurses who volunteered for the trip to establish a first-aid center and dispense necessary medications.

There were 101 patients engaged in the project, but only seventy-four assembled on a Tuesday morning for departure. Twelve of the twenty-seven patients who were left behind were in the groups of two leaders who were unable to make the trip themselves. Those patients had less motivation to go and were permitted to drop out because other leaders preferred not to accept responsibility for patients they were not familiar with. Of the remaining fifteen patients, two flatly refused to leave the hospital; others were ruled out because of frequent episodes of belligerence and acting out that required greater control and supervision than would be available.

The destination of the campers was a YMCA camp at Lake Alpine, about 110 miles away in the Sierra Nevada. The trip to the site was made in chauffeured, rented buses. The ride was a difficult one; because of road construction, it took about five hours. But the vacation spirit carried everyone through in good shape, and the drivers commented that the patients behaved better under the trying circumstances than most passengers they carry. It was necessary to hike the last mile to the camp, and it was gratifying to see the help spontaneously offered by the younger people to the more elderly. This attitude continued throughout the excursion.

Because the camp consisted of ten bunkhouses, it was possible to house the groups as units and permit local autonomy over housekeeping arrangements. The staff expected people to care for their own bedding and maintain some order. However, it was agreed in advance that because the excursion was a holiday, all camp activities should be voluntary. There were about twenty unmade beds the first morning but only about ten later that day. Only six patients routinely left their beds unmade. There were isolated cases of meals missed completely or partly, or eaten in self-imposed seclusion, but the incidents were not repeated.

The washrooms were located about two hundred feet from the bunkhouses, in craggy mountains, with shrubbery creating hazards en route. Stronger campers assisted the less steady ones without being asked, reflecting the general attitude of cooperation. The difficulties with the washrooms may have been an incentive. One of the group leaders said that the early announcement that changes of clothing and bedding were limited was even more of a challenge. In any event, the five patients who had been reported to be regularly incontinent in the hospital did not present that problem during the trip.

The recreational activities for the campers included wading, swimming, boating, hiking, other outdoor sports, and table games. Recreation was particularly successful because patients were permitted to participate freely and spontaneously. There was a sizeable minority who wanted only to *rest;* they did so. The dining and recreation hall was the center for social interaction. The hall had a piano, which often attracted groups of singers. Nobody seemed to miss the television set.

Other diversions included two evening campfires with folk dancing and community singing. Four members of the rehabilitation services came to the camp one evening to lead campfire activities, providing the only break the group leaders had during the five days. They lifted the morale in more than one way; their comment that the project members looked like campers rather than patients was very encouraging to the staff.

Meals were an outstanding feature of the trip. In spite of considerable apprehension about serving food family style, it was a great success. Many campers expressed genuine pleasure about being able to fill their plates with food they selected. When a food was in short supply, word was quickly passed around the table, and the response was spontaneous and unanimously appropriate. At one of the meals there was a real argument about whether such delicious food had been supplied by the institution, and there were many questions about why meals couldn't be managed so well all the time. The staff unanimously cited improved table manners as a major gain of the trip.

It turned out to be hardship for the small staff of eleven to be, in effect, on duty twenty-four hours a day from Tuesday morning to Saturday evening. Patients worked actively on the kitchen crews, both in food preparation and cleanup, and did the camp housekeeping chores, all with little supervision from the staff. The group leaders felt that there were some advantages in the shortage of staff, because patients responded well to being left to their own devices; in general patients saw the need to help with the work and responded heroically. However, the consensus was that on the next trip it would be advisable to provide a few hours of relief for each staff member each day. There was also a consensus, with less conviction, that it would help to engage a professional to administer the kitchen. Because everybody had equal amateur standing in the kitchen, hidden talents of many were discovered.

The camp director, who at first had doubts about leasing the site for mental hospital patients, subsequently wrote to the hospital inviting them to return. Throughout the trip, staff members noted the absence of typical hospital behavior, an observation that has been reported by others on similar expeditions. Even if the improvement were only temporary, it demonstrated the patients' capacity for socially acceptable performance. For instance, one patient who was a constant hand-wringer and hair-twister abstained from that behavior from the time the bus left the hospital until she boarded for the return trip. When she was asked why she started wringing her hands again, she said, "We're going back to the hospital." Another patient appeared for breakfast every morning at camp, although getting her up had been a major problem on the ward, and continues to be so. Several patients who had refused to write to their families for years did so at camp, because post cards are expected from someone on *vacation.* In many cases a gain resulted from family members' awareness that their relative could leave the hospital; there were home visits and family outings for patients who had not had such experiences in years. Another side effect of this trip was the increase in self-referrals to the project by other patients.

Of all the benefits derived from the camping trip, the most lasting and significant appears to be the changed perception of patients by staff. The group leaders continue to talk about incidents in which patients behaved very differently from the way they do under hospital routine. The staff, too, behaved differently outside the confines of the hospital role. They were better able to relinquish control, permitting patients to experience more independence. They were also more likely to interact like people with people, instead of like staff with patients. That, perhaps, was the greatest advantage of the experience.

CHAPTER VI

SOME CAMPING THERAPY PROGRAMS IN INDIANA AND TEXAS

ORA K. ACKERMAN, SPIRO B. MITSOS, A. MARGARET SEYMOUR AND BERT KRUGER SMITH

INDIANA

IN SEPTEMBER OF 1958, two groups of patients from the Evansville State Hospital became the first participants in a camping experience which promises to become a regular part of the hospital's activities program.

This was a joint venture, with the hospital providing the staff, food, linens and general supplies, and the Indiana Association for Mental Health furnishing funds for the rental of the camp as well as for incidental expenses, including camp clothing and pin money for the patients.

The camp site is located at Lincoln State Park some forty miles distant from the hospital. Facilities include a large dining-recreation building, groups of sleeping cabins, an infirmary, a central shower house, staff cabins and an office. Sleeping cabins are arranged in four units with each unit having three cabins and each cabin accommodating twelve to fourteen campers. Each unit has its own toilet facilities and a separate staff cabin. However, in our case none of the staff cabins were used as the entire staff shared sleeping quarters with the campers.

Sixteen staff members from the hospital were involved in the camp project. The coordinator of activity therapies was camp director, with the director of occupational therapy serving as assistant camp director. The remainder of the staff consisted of nine members of the activity therapy department, two registered nurses, two attendants and the camp chef, an employee of the dietary department.

Patients selected to attend the camp were carefully screened and selected by different criteria each week. The first week's campers were a group of younger convalescing acute patients. Campers for the second week were selected from the older chronic patients, with special emphasis on two points: (1) they must be working patients deserving of a vacation, and (2) they must be patients having few or no visits from relatives or friends.

Because it was intended that the camp would be a place of few restrictions and ample freedom, there were no locked doors anywhere. Instead, an imaginary boundary was set up and within this area campers were free to go where they pleased when they were not in an organized activity. To our knowledge no camper abused this privilege.

Besides caring for his own personal hygiene, each camper had several regular assignments and duties to perform each day. He was responsible for making his bed and helping keep his cabin clean. On a scheduled basis members of the various cabins were responsible to all other campers for preparation of meals, serving meals, or cleaning up. In all of these aspects of the camp activities, staff and campers worked together.

The recreation and craft programs ran concurrently and incorporated different activities each day. The composition of the groups themselves also changed daily. This was easily accomplished since none of the specific projects were of such magnitude as to require more than one of the craft periods.

Campers Participate Freely

In both recreation and craft activities, in fact in the entire camping enterprise, the most encouraging factor was the camper participation. At no point in the program was anybody forced to participate, but nearly every one took part in the various programs. Emphasis was placed on having each camper experience as great a variety of activities as possible.

Probably the best indication of the success of the initial camping project is the fact that no consideration has been given to not repeating it. Plans have been under way since March for this year's program, which is expected to differ from last year's only in regard to personal freedom. The consensus is that last year's schedule was a little too tight, and that a relaxing of the planned activities will enhance the therapeutic experience.

TEXAS

More than five hundred patients have already been privileged to share in the Texas state hospital camping program which began in 1956. Now an annual event under the sponsorship of the hospital board, this has become an exciting and promising new development in the state's rehabilitation programs.

The camp site was made available without charge to the state hospital system, as it is to other worthwhile endeavors, by the H. E. Butt Foundation. Mrs. Eleanor Bird, rehabilitation therapist for the Kerrville State Home, was named director of the camp. Her many years of camping experience and her unquenchable belief in the camping project have been largely responsible for its successful continuation.

The selection of patients and of personnel was quickly recognized as the most vital ingredient in conducting the program. Persons responsible for the camp regard as essential the careful screening of patients to select those ready to test their skills in living, skills which can best be tried in a protected situation away from the hospitals. In no sense is the camp regarded as a *vacation site* for long-term patients nor as a rest for those who have worked faithfully in the hospitals. Rather, it is a proving ground for living.

Authorities recognize that a patient cannot test himself fully inside the protective arms of the hospital, nor is he always certain enough of himself to move directly from hospital to the strains of home and community living. But at camp, which might be considered a stepping-stone toward home, the patient can test himself in true democratic living, while at the same time having the protection provided by trained personnel and the camp setting. For the first two years of the program thirty patients from each of the six Texas hospitals, two hospital groups at a time, came for a one-week stay. During the third year this was increased to ten days.

A permanent camp staff has been made available, with the hospitals providing a doctor, cabin counselors, a safety counselor, a rehabilitation therapist and food service personnel. Camp personnel attend a two-day workshop before the arrival of the patients in order that they can learn about camp facilities and can discuss and evaluate techniques of group work in a camp setting.

What Do These Days at Camp Mean to the Patients Themselves?

Reluctance is often their first reaction, unwillingness to go from the protection of the hospital, hesitation at leaving the nurse or attendant who has become a sort of mother figure, reluctance to make decisions again. The trip itself in a big, modern bus is often a frightening experience for patients who have been on hospital grounds for many years.

Sometimes on the bus trip they sit rigid, turning their heads from the unfamiliar scenery, fearful of noisy streets and careening cars. They fight what they do not know. Gradually the movement of the bus, the sight of trees and tangled wild flowers, the spotted cows munching grass begin to bring peace into their bodies.

Still many of the fears remain. As the bus turns into the sloping road to the camp, many of the patients regain their uncertainties at the sight of the narrow road and sharp curves. At this moment the camping program begins. Mrs. Bird, her blue eyes alive with laughter, steps into the bus and rides the remainder of the way with the group, enthusiastically telling stories of exploits along the old wagon trail on which they are traveling, laughing with delight as the bus lumbers into the river bottom, its huge tires splashing water over the rocks.

From that moment on the group becomes campers, not patients. They are never referred to as patients as long as they remain in camp.

Finally they step stiffly from the bus and look around, viewing the tree-clothed hills, the cabins and main lodge of rustic stone, the scrub oaks bathing their feet in the Frio River.

They hear the underbreath of wind humming through the canyon. They see the river licking gently at the rocky banks; they feel the earth, still warm with remembrance of summer. They smell the pungent smoke of wood, and they taste the crusty skin of potatoes roasted over an open fire. Thus are all five senses newly brought to remembrance of past wonder and latent beauty.

The setting itself is therapeutic. A middle-aged man whose twenty years on the farm still show in the sun-squint lines around his eyes crumbles the earth between his hands and feels once again its promise. A young girl who has been inside the hospital for five years sees the water and is washed with remembrance of cleanliness and joy. And an older woman sits quietly on the sun-spotted terrace and warms herself with the peace and stillness of the moment.

Personnel Also Enjoy Camping

This almost magical transformation comes not only to the patients, but to the personnel. In this non-institutional setting, without their uniforms, away from hospital pressures, they also become campers. Now they can give leadership to patient-campers only when necessary and can work with them in a person-to-person role.

Patient-campers are shown to their cabins, each one housing fifteen persons from the two hospitals plus a camp counselor. They unpack their boxes carefully, looking around the big room, delighting in the corner fireplace, smelling the air of freedom. At dinner the first night the camp director explains the principles of camping, and the democratic process begins. Councilwomen or councilmen are elected from each cabin and they begin to sit in on decision-making about future activities. There are no rigid assignments concerning programming but rather a truly democratic choice of group activities and duties, the latter consisting of cabin cleaning and helping with the kitchen chores.

No doors are locked—no two days are the same. Ten simple

words which spell a change in life, in outlook and in feeling for people who have listened for hundreds of nights to the sound of keys turning in locks, who have awakened in the morning to the knowledge of a one colored life filled with routine.

To some the activities; fishing, hiking, swimming, games, singing, provide the greatest experience. To others the blessed joy of sitting alone under a tree and watching the simple grace of a spotted fawn, the proud tramping of a wild turkey, the setting sun spilling its red-gold beauty on the canyon brings release of spirit.

The buddy system is used at all times, and no accidents have occurred at camp. Each activity is a miracle to the campers and a tribute to the personnel. The mere act of providing swimming in the Frio River takes both ingenuity and vigilance. A waterfront counselor is on hand at all times, and dozens of campers who have not known the joy of swimming for years are buoyed up by both the water and a sense of well-being.

An older man who said, "I never thought I'd fish again," takes the fishing poles in his thin, veined hand, and is happy as he has not been for years. Hiking through the hills, participating in sing-songs and fish fries bring to these campers a renewed sense of life's goodness and their own worth.

Herman might serve as an example of what the camping program can do for patients. In the hospital and when he first came to camp, he was mute and uncooperative. As he started fishing, he also began talking with the other campers. At the end of his week at camp, he was voted the *Camper Who Had Improved the Most.* As he left camp, he remarked to the director, "Say, if I can get along with people like this, I could do it back home." Before long Herman was discharged from the hospital and is now holding a job in his community.

Or take Linda, a former school teacher who had been in the hospital for eleven years, much of the time combative and confined to a back ward. Tranquilizing drugs had helped her, though she arrived at camp still fearful. The first night, sitting around the camp fire, she sang a solo. From then on her progress was remarkable. "I know I can get along with people," she said,

"I know I can plan." Within a month she was discharged from the hospital and had made plans to return to college for some refresher courses.

Dr. Cyril J. Ruilmann, medical director for the Texas state hospitals, has said of the camping program:

> "I have great faith in the ability of this program to provide for many patients a unique kind of interpersonal relationship which plays a real part in preparing the patients to return to the community. I would like to see the program expanded to the degree that every patient who could profit from it could be allowed all the time he or she needed in the camp experience."

CHAPTER VII

THERAPEUTIC CAMPING FOR MARYLAND'S CHRONIC MENTAL PATIENTS

MAXWELL N. WEISMAN, LENORA MANN AND BEN W. BARKER

SOCIAL CRIPPLING, while often the cause of mental hospitalization by an intolerant society, is even more often the product of the very agency whose therapeutic goal is rehabilitation for return to society. Already struggling with his own internal forces of disintegration and depersonalization, the chronic mental patient in the course of years of hospitalization finds himself immured in institutional mores which gradually drain him of whatever strength and hope for health he ever had. Separated from his normal associations, deprived of the need or even the right to solve many of his problems, prevented from making even the simplest decisions, and enervated by boredom in the empty and meaningless world of the back ward, he sooner or later falls prey to social crippling.

Constituting between sixty-five and seventy-five percent of the hospital population, this hard-core group of continued care patients is the cause of grave concern to those who wish to reduce the hospital population and convert the state mental hospital into a comprehensive, intensive treatment center. Obviously, the needs of these patients differ from those of the newly admitted. Having accepted hospital residence as a way of life, beginning with broken family ties and the severance of relationships generally, this patient finds himself dependent on others, who tell him when and what he must eat, when to go to bed, rise and bathe, and what clothes to wear. Time, the newspapers, and the community mean little to him.

To break through this cycle of isolation and withdrawal, the

Maryland Department of Mental Hygiene has recently instituted a residential camp program for its long-stay patients. The department sees this as only one of several new approaches needed to restore these long-term patients to productivity and community living.

ORIGINS OF THERAPEUTIC CAMPING

Organized camping in the United States has passed the century mark since the founding of the first school camp in 1861 (Ward). Even the private camp movement for children can trace its roots back as far as 1890, when the first such educational camp was opened for the sons of the well-to-do (Mitchell). Of much more recent origin, however, is the camping movement for physically handicapped and emotionally disturbed children, and for the mentally ill adult it is even more recent.

McNeil notes that the literature on camping was almost entirely free from references to "psychology," "character" or "mental hygiene" until the 1930's when the growth of the fields of psychology, social work, and education had an important impact on the theory and practice of camping (McNeil). By 1937, Blumenthal was able to state that camping, from such early objectives as "fresh air" outings for the poor boys or a wholesome "outdoors" alternative for the rich boy who might otherwise idle his summer away in the sophistication of a resort hotel, had now arrived at the "threshold of a social, mental hygiene objective of the adequate personality functioning successfully in group living" (Blumenthal).

Papers followed each other on camping for the hard-of-hearing (Luther), the diabetic (Clarke), the crippled (Marx), the blind (Nickelsburg), the cardiac (Sellwood), the handicapped generally (Ash, Backus, Crawford, Decker, DiClemente, Goodwin, Howett), the juvenile delinquent (Breed, Close, Moeller, Weber), and the disturbed child (Hallowitz, Middleman, Tilley).

This new camping philosophy aimed at providing the child with a social setting under adult guidance which would expressly solidify psychological and emotional maturity. Harms, in fact, spoke of "camps as mental health institutions" in an issue of *The Nervous Child* in 1947 which was devoted to the "Psychopathology and psychotherapy of camping" (Harms). Papers were included by Redl on "The psychopathologic risks of camp life," Gumprecht on "Common emotional disturbances of children at camp," Perlman on "Camps for maladjusted children," and Eells on "Camp as a therapeutic community."

Camping programs for the mentally ill adult, however, have been described only within the last ten years in Tennessee (Peterson), Connecticut (Bergan, Devlin), Indiana (Ackerman), Texas (Smith), and Maryland (Chestnut Lodge) (George). (The authors are also aware of more recent programs in other states, such as North Dakota, which have not yet appeared in the professional journals.)

PLANNING A SOCIAL TREATMENT CAMP PROGRAM

Following the lead of these pioneer programs, the Maryland Department of Mental Hygiene decided to apply the fundamental principles of a social treatment program within a camp setting and providing a greater opportunity for patients to be creative, expressive, and responsible, even allowing for freedom of choice in such important things as how the patient likes his breakfast eggs cooked. Respect for the dignity, integrity, and abilities of all individuals would be basic.

To create a freer atmosphere, plans were made to remove signs of hospital authority; no keys, uniforms, or titles. Staff and patients would be on as equal a footing as possible; eating at the same tables, observing the same camp rules, sleeping in the same type of beds, and generally maintaining the same type of schedules.

These were the thoughts expressed by a central camp committee, appointed by the commissioner to plan and direct the implementation of the camp program. The director of rehabilitation of the central office was chairman of the committee, which also included the director of community psychiatric services and the director of food services. Other members were: two social workers (the germ of the camp idea came from one of them); a recreational therapist, who had previous camp experience with mental patients; and the clinical director of one of the larger hospitals in the state. Soon after the first meeting, the committee was enlarged to include one liaison member from each of the four participating hospitals, since hospital intercommunication and follow-up of the committee's plans were necessary.

Two co-directors for the camp were selected: one, a social worker with previous professional experience in camping had the over-all responsibility for administration; the other, the recreational therapist mentioned above, was responsible for program activities. Subcommittees with specific functions were formed to select personnel, draft a flexible activity program, outline medical procedures, establish criteria for the selection of patients, handle food requirements and other housekeeping necessities, and outline post-camp procedures.

Two two-week periods were agreed upon, each including forty-eight patients. Each of the four participating hospitals was requested to select twelve patients between the ages of forty and sixty who had been hospitalized for a period of at least two years, had reached a plateau in their hospitalization process, and were seemingly unmotivated for further progress. Men and women would be in equal numbers. Program planning, it was felt, would be more effective if the group was homogeneous in age and degree of chronicity.

Further criteria were that patients be able to care for personal needs, be physically able to participate in an active program, and be free of symptoms that would create serious management problems. These criteria did not eliminate the patient who was still overtly psychotic, and there were many who showed delusionary behavior of different kinds. Thus, in terms of display of symptoms and degree of chronicity, patients selected for the camp project represented a cross section of patient populations from the four participating hospitals. On the whole, appropriate selections were made, although this is an area in which we need additional study as indicated below. Actually, many of the patients selected had been hospitalized for close to thirty years.

A children's camp with several acres of wooded land and a running mountain stream was found, owned and operated by the Lutheran Social Services of Maryland, Inc., and available in September after the children left. It included six cabins for eight each, an outdoor swimming pool, a large lodge containing a dining room, kitchen, first-aid stations, craft rooms, and a laundry. The rental arrangement also included the use of bedding, telephone service, a station wagon, and the services of a full-time camp caretaker.

The hospitals provided their own dietary staff (one cook, two kitchen helpers), each team operating for one week. Food stores for the most part were drawn from one state hospital, with the cost shared among the four hospitals. Because there were perishables, a refrigerated truck for the transportation of all foodstuffs was rented at a modest cost. The cost for the use of the camp was $1.80 per day for each person involved (patients and staff). Since there were no budgeted or state-appropriated funds for this program, each hospital appealed to auxiliaries and other volunteer groups and had little difficulty in raising $1,000.

RECRUITMENT OF STAFF PERSONNEL

All personnel to operate the camp, recruited by the two codirectors, as well as patients were to volunteer for the program. One registered nurse was to be on duty at all times in the event first-aid treatment was needed. General practitioners in the surrounding community were advised of our impending program and agreed to be on call.

Staff members recruited from the participating hospitals quickly formed a cohesive working group. Since their participation was voluntary because the work involved overtime with no compensation, it was clear that only those devoted to this type of program and skilled in recreation activity would volunteer. Coupled with their experience in working with psychiatric patients, this gave them a common base from which to function. They met for two training sessions in advance of camp. The first was a general discussion of the program and structure of the camp and took place in one of the hospitals. The second was a cookout at the camp site.

Most of those serving as program specialists in charge of an activity, such as crafts, nature activity, and swimming, were from rehabilitation departments. Cabin counselors, who lived with the campers and assisted in program activities, were members of nursing services with two exceptions (a rehabilitation therapist and a social work student).

On the whole, the staff was dedicated to the job. They were with the campers at all times and participated freely in activity with them. First names were used by campers and staff alike and this did much to break down the hierarchy so often found in hospitals. The first day of camp one of the campers remarked to two counselors, members of nursing personnel, that when she first arrived she thought the two counselors were nurses there to supervise her. Asked what she now thought they were, the camper replied, "Why, patients, just like me."

A problem with some counselors involved doing too much for campers, rather than helping them do for themselves. This was evident in such things as making decorations or costumes where the counselor's greater skill could produce a result more quickly and effectively. Another area of concern was their fear of the camper's being injured and thus not permitting him to take risks such as scalding the dishes or tending the cookout fire. When it was suggested they teach the camper to do it safely, the response was invariably that they feared he would be hurt, a reaction probably stemming from fear of disciplinary action in the hospital when a patient is injured.

PATIENT EXPERIENCES IN AN OUTDOOR SETTING

Camp living routines, as well as program activities, were planned to meet the needs of the chronic, regressed schizophrenic. The cabin counselor shared responsibility with the group of eight campers for performing daily work assignments such as cleaning, table-setting, and dishwashing. The pace was deliberately slow, with ample time allowed for the performance of work chores. Many had lost (or had never learned) such skills as setting a table properly. Time had to be allowed, therefore, for teaching. Hands unused to labor of any kind had to be retrained. Social graces, such as waiting to eat until grace was said and remaining at table until all were finished, had to be relearned. Many found security in performing the simple tasks of setting and clearing the table. Others found satisfaction in the daily chore of cutting firewood for the large fireplace. Still others, taking renewed pride in personal appearance, learned to operate the washing machine and dryer.

Food, its serving and handling, as well as its content, touches deep emotional needs and was capitalized upon. Mealtimes were leisurely. Food was good. Cooks, recruited from hospital kitchens and accustomed to mass feeding, soon came to enjoy preparing special food treats. For example, campers ate the first fried eggs they had had since hospitalization, as well as pancakes and French toast. Coffee was available between meals, as were materials for popping corn and making fudge.

It was interesting to note, however, that only rarely did groups pop corn or make fudge on their own initiative. Usually a staff member had to suggest and direct these activities. Undoubtedly, part of the hesitancy came from the lack of initiative resulting from the long years of inactivity. An equally valid reason was the trouble involved. Women forgot how to measure a cup of sugar and had to be urged to continue filling until the cup was level. It was tedious to stand over the pot and watch the cooking time. Popping corn required squatting by a hot fire for a long period of time and was uncomfortable. Thus, if someone else would make it, all would enjoy eating it. But, left to their own initiative, they would do without.

A small canteen was operated, stocked with cigarettes, candy, gum, and stamps. The camp had a soft drink vending machine. Hospitals issued five dollars' spending money to each camper, which provided another type of learning experience. For many, this was the first money of their own in years and some spent it all in the first week. In the Maryland state system, a limited number of letters may be mailed by patients at state expense. Thus, they never have occasion to purchase a stamp, so it was not surprising that few knew the cost of postage.

Helping campers to deal with these realities of life outside the hospital was a continuous challenge for the staff. One man whose allowance was issued to him at camp could not believe that all that money could be for him. He immediately bought a package of cigarettes, and became quite disturbed at having to give up a quarter, incorporating the experience into his delusional system. In the swimming pool a short time later, he was seen sitting in a shallow corner actively hallucinating about people stealing his money.

Within the framework of these living routines and experiences, we offered activities that would further stimulate forgotten memories. None of the hospitals from which these people came had a swimming pool, but the camp did. There was a stream running through camp so that fishing was a part of the program. The camp was surrounded by wooded hills and hiking became the most popular activity. The crafts counselor capitalized on the interest in nature and geared most craft projects to those which would use natural materials. These activities were offered morning and afternoon, with campers given a choice of which they would do.

The emphasis was always on helping campers use individual and group initiative. This concept presupposes that opportunity will be provided for individuals and small groups to plan projects beyond the narrow limits of a preplanned program. While we considered this a desirable goal, we were forced to accept the fact that two weeks was not time enough to help long hospitalized patients achieve this goal beyond a minimal level. Scheidlinger states:

> The principle of self-determination which is used in social work needs to be thoughtfully applied with groups that are made up of emotionally-disturbed members. Self-determination implies a "self" that can participate in decision making. The group worker must do much of the initial planning and help the group achieve satisfaction in order for the group to assume any responsibility for the planning at later stages (Scheidlinger).

New experiences, disconcerting for normal groups, could immobilize psychiatric patients. At the beginning of an activity period, all campers were called together and asked to separate into groups according to their choice of activity. Some chose with sureness, but most had to be asked individually which activity he preferred. This pattern continued into the second week of each session, and it was not until this time that individuals showed evidence of having thought in advance about what they would do. This is the point at which groups can be helped to plan new activity, using beginning experiences as a base. We were able to achieve this only minimally within the time left in the camp period by increasing the tempo of all activities and by planning special events such as a carnival, a tournament of games, or a talent show.

EVALUATION OF THE CAMP SESSIONS

The fact that any degree of progress could be noted in the group's functioning in a two-week time period is sound evidence of the value of this type of program for chronic patients. While we have no really scientific measure of progress, we have valid observations of individual growth. A talent show was the culminating activity of each session and vividly demonstrated increased capacity to relate to others in what could be a threatening situation. Most performances in the show were crude renditions of a song. Yet each performer faced the group with confidence that his contribution would be accepted, as indeed it was. In one of the shows, a deaf mute spontaneously demanded the floor to perform a dramatic interpretation of a battle scene. The ovation he received was evidence of the group's recognition of his wish to contribute, as well as to their appreciation of his effort.

Campers verbalized a sense of release in many ways, from one woman's comment the first day, with arms flung wide, "This is freedom!" to another's remark, "Gosh, we are doing anything we want—no supervision or anything." There was much more talk of families and of things that happened before hospitalization than is usual on the hospital ward. One may conjecture that this is due, at least in part, to the sudden shift to a completely open setting and to a society in which self-assertion is the expectation.

A woman hospitalized for many years, flat in affect, diagnosed schizophrenic, catatonic type, began talking of her former home in Baltimore. Gradually she wondered whether her key would still fit the apartment and announced that she would get back there some way. She eventually eloped from camp and was found in the vicinity of her old address. The camp experience was no doubt responsible not only for the reawakened interest in her previous life but for the new-found initiative to do something about it.

What is basically involved is the acceptance of healthy behavior as the norm and the expected. Where the effects of hospitalization contribute overwhelmingly to identification as a *patient,* deviant behavior becomes normal and normal behavior deviant. A typical case is Padula's report (Padula) of a young patient who for years in a V.A. hospital walked backward. Nevertheless, the hospital readied him for a trial visit to his home. A nurse happened to see him in the street walking normally and asked him in amazement how he had been able to change. "Oh," he replied, "on the outside you are not allowed to walk backward."

Campers found new ways of channeling energies. A woman, aged twenty-seven and an exception to the age limit because of her regression in four years of hospitalization, was described by her psychiatrist as follows:

> Patient is a very industrious worker, appearing to absorb all her energies in her work as a means of attempting to stay here in the hospital. She socializes poorly with the other patients and on occasions, if too much pressure is placed on her, is apt to get angry.

At camp, Mrs. B. was extremely hostile to staff during the first week and unrelated to the rest of the camper group. Gradually she became active in the program and communicative toward others. A vacancy occurred in the second session and, because of her improvement, she was returned for an additional session. She still absorbed much energy in work assignments, but was helped by staff to take a leadership role in her cabin in teaching newcomers how to do things. In this role there was improvement in her relation to those in authority, as well as to her peers.

One man, eight years in the hospital, intelligent and in good contact, had evaded every attempt to get him to leave the hospital. On the last day of camp, he tried to express his appreciation for the camp experience to a social worker on the staff by saying,

> "You can't know what it meant to me the other day to find myself in the pool with you. In the past, I have been so angry toward social workers, psychiatrists, and all the others and this experience has helped break down most of that feeling."

Shortly after camp, he was able to be discharged from the hospital.

Sometimes improvement took place when we could not see it. One camper spent all of his five dollars' allowance on soft drinks within the first few days he was there. After this, he frequented the vending machine, punching buttons in the hope that a bottle would drop. This appeared to be the most productive activity of which he was capable, as most of the time he sat withdrawn from the group and participated only marginally in any activity. When there was an opportunity for a male patient to return to camp for a second session, nursing personnel on his ward asked that he be allowed to come. We refused this, because staff who knew him best felt he had gained nothing from the first session experience. However, a few months after the camping period he was cited as one who had sustained the greatest gain from camp. Whereas he had never talked on the ward before, he now asked for everything he needed.

While many more cases of improvement in individuals could be cited, there were also failures when campers could not adjust to the sudden change. Some regressed steadily during camp and continued the regression when returned to the hospital. One woman had been nude and incontinent, but improved enough to warrant being sent to camp. Upon arrival, she tore her dress and lay down on the ground. She said she wanted to stay, but was unable to tolerate clothes or upright posture. She had to be sent back to the hospital on the return bus. A man with uncouth personal habits seemed unable to relate in any way except to beg cigarettes. His behavior was intolerable to campers and staff alike and, since all efforts of the staff to help him failed, he was returned to the hospital. Another man set a brush fire near the woods and investigation showed he had a history of fire-setting, although there had been no evidence of this in recent years.

Some with behavior problems worse than those noted above were able to tolerate camp and to show improvement. Many were delusional part of the time; some of these were disturbing to others and some were not. Approximately seventy-five percent of all campers were diagnosed schizophrenic with the remainder divided among mental deficiency, psychotic depression, and chronic brain syndromes. Diagnosis does not provide the answer to what kind of patients respond to camp, however, as good and bad experiences could be cited from any one classification. We need to know more about how to select patients for camp and/or how to prepare them for the experience so that the impact of the sudden change will be less traumatic.

A total of ninety patients participated fully in the camp program. Within three months after returning to the hospital, forty-one were able to be discharged and a year later all but two of these were still living in the community.

Efforts are now being made to evaluate the factors which may have been involved in effecting these discharges among a group of patients who had not been able to respond positively to the other programs conducted within the hospital.

REFERENCES

Ackerman, O. R.; Mitsos, S. B., and Seymour, A. M.: Patients go camping in Indiana, *Ment Hosp, 10:*16-17, 1959.

Ash, F.: Sometimes the handicapped give more than they receive, *Camping Magazine, 7:*11, 1945.

Backus, R.: Suggested standards for camp referrals of physically handicapped children, *Camping Magazine, 17:*15, 1945.

Bergan, J. F.: Day camp in Connecticut, *Ment Hosp, 9:*12-13, 1958.

Blumenthal, L. H.: *Group Work in Camping,* New York: Association Press, 1937.

Breed, A. F.: "California youth authority forestry camp program," in Glueck, S. (ed): *The Problem of Delinquency.* Boston: Houghton Mifflin Co., pp. 705-711, 1959.

Clarke, A.: Camps for diabetic children, *Camping Magazine, 9:*10, 1937.

Close, O. H.: California camps for delinquents, in Bell, M. (ed): *Social Correctives for Delinquency.* New York National Probation and Parole Association, pp. 136-147, 1946.

Crawford, M.: Provide the handicapped with a rich camp experience, *Camping Magazine, 28:*18, 1956.

Decker, S., and Herzog, J.: More camping for children with handicaps, *Camping Magazine, 30:*26, 1958.

Devlin, E. W., and Irvine, L. M., Jr.: Camping with the mentally ill adult: A new dimension, paper presented at the National Conference on Social Welfare, Los Angeles, Calif., 1964.

DiClemente, H.: Try riflery with handicapped campers, *Camping Magazine, 28:*16, 1956.

George, G. R., and Gibson, R. W.: Patient-Staff relationships change with environment, *Ment Hosp, 10:*18-19, 1959.

Goodwin, H., and Cross, E.: How handicapped campers can fit into regular programs, *Camping Magazine, 30:*18, 1958.

Hallowitz, E.: Camping for disturbed children, *Ment Hyg, 34:*406-422, 1950.

Harms, E.: Camps as mental health institutions, *Nerv Child, 6:*127, 1947.

Howett, H.: Workshop on camping for the handicapped, *Camping Magazine, 17:*21, 1945.

Luther, R.: Outdoor happiness for the hard-of-hearing, *Camping Magazine, 10:*15, 1938.

Marx, E.: Camping for crippled children, *Camping Magazine, 16:*5, 1944.

Marx, E.: Camping for crippled children, *Camping Magazine, 16:*15, 1944.

McNeil, E. B.: The background of therapeutic camping, *J Soc Issues, 13:*4, 1957.

Middleman, R., and Seever, F.: Short-term camping for boys with behavior problems, *Soc Work, 8:*88-89, 1963.

Mitchell, V., and Crawford, I.: *Camp Counseling.* Philadelphia, W. B. Saunders Co., 1950.

Moeller, H. G.: The natural bridge camp, in Bell, M. (ed): *Bulwarks Against Crime.* New York, National Probation and Parole Association, pp. 162-173, 1949.

Nickelsburg, J.: Even the blind can see nature, *Camping Magazine, 21:*14, 1949.

Padula, H.: Releasing the human potential in chronic mental patients through social work services, *Soc Worker, 29:*13-25, 1961.

Peterson, B. F.: An experiment in living, *Ment Hosp, 6:*8-9, 1955.

Scheidlinger, S., et al.: Social group work on psychiatric residential settings, *Am J Orthopsychiatry, 26:*724, 1956.

Sellwood, J. J.: Camping for cardiac children, *Camping Magazine, 30:*20, 1955.

Smith, B. K.: Patients go camping in Texas, *Ment Hosp, 10:*17-18, 1959.

Tilley, P. L.: The in-camp adjustment of three different types of problem behavior boys at the University of Michigan Fresh Air Camp, unpublished master's thesis, University of Michigan School of Education, 1948.

Ward, C. E.: *Organized Camping and Progressive Education.* Nashville, Informal Education Service, 1935, p. 4.

Weber, G. H.: *Camps for Delinquent Boys, A Guide to Planning.* Washington, D.C.: Government Printing Office, Children's Bureau Publication No. 385, 1960.

CHAPTER VIII

CAMPING AT A SHORT TERM PRIVATE PSYCHIATRIC HOSPITAL

Thomas P. Lowry

Most of what is written about psychiatric camping therapy emphasizes rehabilitation and remotivation of long-term chronic, institutionalized patients. The following program is part of the therapy at Ross General Hospital, in Ross, California. This proprietary hospital nestles among great trees, at the base of a wooded hill, in a wealthy suburb. Most patients have their care paid by private funds or insurance; a few public patients are treated under contract. The average length of stay is eleven days.

But patient wealth and rapid discharge are not panaceas, and several of us despaired of the impotence of hospital psychiatry in *reaching* certain patients. Some patients hid behind a facade of tightness and control; others lost portions of their already-low self-esteem because their needs were too fully met by the hospital kitchen and housekeeping staff. Still others, whose fragile egos made contact slowly seemed unable to blossom because of the brevity of an eight-hour nursing shift and the interruptions of hospital routine. We envied the advantages of marathon groups, with their persistence and timelessness; we envied the Joshua Bierer and Synanon organizations because of their superb utilization of healthy group pressures. We knew the difficulties of breaking the mold of the conventional hospital setting, with its advantages and customs.

It came to several of us simultaneously that a solution would be brief camping outings, where we could create the new situation, without getting involved in challenging the present structure of psychiatry, where the medical model and the patient's insurance policy clauses govern so much of what we do.

GENERAL SETTING

A twenty-four bed, unlocked psychiatric wing of a 235 bed general hospital. The three most common diagnoses are depression, schizophrenia, and alcoholism. The psychiatric unit has the well-known features of an intensive-care program: daily group therapy, occupational therapy, a psychiatric social worker, evening meetings for patients' families, Alcoholics Anonymous, dance therapy, group cooking sessions, somatic therapies, outings to stores and museums, mental health films, visits to Synanon and Recovery, Inc., individual sessions with the patient's personal psychiatrist, and continuous liaison between director, nurses, and medical staff.

PROCEDURE

In northern California, it rains about five months of the year. This makes winter camping impractical because of the additional equipment needed and the physically weakened condition of many depressives and alcoholics.

Trips are scheduled when the patient group and the weather both seem suitable. Each year, we have had about seven overnight trips. We announce trips about five days in advance at a ward group meeting. Through a process of selection and staff encouragement, with the approval of the patient's own psychiatrist, we assemble a workable group. This group then meets daily to plan menus, calculate food amounts, order from the hospital kitchen, arrange camping gear and discuss camping sites. The number of patients on a trip has ranged from two (due to last-minute emergencies) to ten. The staff members who go have all asked to be included. We usually have two staff members: a female occupational therapist, and a female nurse. Dress is informal; there are no uniforms.

We usually choose a campsite accessible by car, with potable water. Little effort is made to find *improvements* such as fireplaces or picnic tables. The work at the campsite is divided by necessity and ability; staff-patient distinctions become almost nil. The afternoon activities are usually self-selected; hiking, bird watching, volleyball, and relaxed conversation are typical. In the evening, there is meal preparation, supper and cleanup. After this, there is usually singing and conversation, until each person is ready for sleep.

The staff's role is to be constantly alert to trends in the patient's thinking and behavior, reinforcing socially useful behavior and diverting, ignoring or inhibiting harmful behavior and bizarre thoughts. There are no set rules, since the usual duration of a trip (twenty-six hours) contains so many combinations of interactions. The patients supervise their own medications.

RESULTS

The traditional statistical procedures and computations do not apply here. The numbers are too small, the time too brief, and our sample too biased to be statistically reliable. (We must add that the same defense is made by enormous community programs, when they are asked "to show results.") Our results are what we see transpire, as true participant-observers, weighing this against similar or the same patients in a traditional setting, observed by the same staff. Some general trends seem clear. The further, in time and distance, that the patients get from the hospital, the *saner* they become. The group becomes steadily more cohesive; working and talking together grows *pari passu.* Many patients have requested discharge as soon as they return to the hospital. A sense of closeness persists, and returned campers share an *esprit de corps* for days after their return.

The possibilities of even a brief camping experience may be shown by the following vignettes:

> A 24-year-old schizophrenic salesman had talked constantly of "being sick." During the trip, he became more assertive and less concerned about his symptoms.
>
> A 50-year-old depressed housewife was not willing to talk with others in the hospital. During the trip, she developed much more rapport and became closer and more cooperative.
>
> A 36-year-old housewife, acutely schizophrenic with grandiose delusions, continued some of her compulsive behavior and thoughts but was far more cooperative than she had been at home.
>
> A 22-year-old schizophrenic college student had been extremely withdrawn and isolated in the hospital. On the trip he was able to talk about himself for long periods of time, took on himself the or-

ganization of cooking a large meal and felt quite proud of himself afterward. As he adapted better, the group was very supportive of him.

A 53-year-old housewife with meprobamate addiction and serious depression went on the first camping trip in her life with many misgivings. She took much responsibility in cooking and cleaning, stopped talking about her symptoms, and seemed considerably more relaxed.

A 46-year-old doctor's wife, with many years of sleeping pill addiction, became enraged when she found that the staff had forgotten to pack her sleeping pills. When they refused to drive forty miles to the nearest town to get some more, she had a tantrum, settled down, and for the first time in a decade was able to clearly face the depth of her addiction.

A 63-year-old man in a manic psychosis became gradually calmer and more responsible, dropping many of his grandiose delusions.

A 25-year-old student became frightened and delusional during the night but was reassured, went back to sleep, and was pleased the next morning to find that he had spent the night in the woods without going to pieces.

PROBLEMS

California laws for working women prohibit payment for more than eight hours out of twenty-four. We solved this by compensatory time off. One patient managed to get on a trip without her psychoanalyst's permission. When he arrived at the hospital for their fifty-minute hour, she was gone and he was furious. At his insistence, we dispatched a car to the mountain top where she was camped and returned her. This illustrates the value of advance clarification, to reduce harmful (to the patient) conflict between professionals. Another patient became highly agitated when she met her former lover at a beach. He was also psychotic. She had to return to the hospital. One trip was rained out; the reaction of staff and patients to this was a learning experience and a focus for continued discussion. Other than these incidents, there have been no negative reactions.

CONCLUSION

Providing there is a motivated staff, any institution can utilize camping as a help in the therapy of acutely psychotic patients. The camping program has been carried out with no new costs and with very encouraging results at a small hospital with patient stays of only eleven days.

CHAPTER IX

CAMPING AT A PSYCHIATRIC DAY CENTER

E. EDWARD REITMAN AND ALEX D. POKORNY

ON A SEPTEMBER morning in 1965 the doors to the Houston Veterans Administration Day Treatment Center were closed. For the next seven days, twenty-five patients and twelve staff members spent their time 300 miles away, at a ranch camp in the beautiful, rugged hill country of West Texas.

Although therapeutic camping has been used for mental hospital inpatients for several decades, and several good accounts of it are available, we have not seen any description of such a program for day center patients. Our experience indicates that day patients and inpatients differ in the ways in which they approach a camping trip.

Most of the patients in our day center program, usually numbering about forty-five, are chronic schizophrenics. It is well known that long-term hospitalization tends to foster desocialization in schizophrenic patients. In recent years it has been possible to discharge many of them from the hospital, but mere discharge is not enough. Discharged chronic patients often just sit around at home, not venturing out to take part in work or play, and usually live constricted and routine lives.

For these chronic schizophrenics the day center, with its all-day program and its focus on activities and the therapeutic community, would seem almost ideal, combining as it does most of the advantages of hospital treatment and living at home. But few of these patients are interested in or accessible to psychotherapy. Even at the center they tend to settle into a new set of ruts: they follow routines and rigid schedules, use the same travel routes to and from the center, and engage in habitual activities. They set up a living routine almost as limited as if they were still in the hospital.

For this reason part of our day center program moves them out into the community, to take field trips or use community recreational and educational facilities. We place emphasis on teaching them social skills and exposing them to new experiences. Staff and patients participate in activities in a group. The patients are shown what is possible, interesting, enjoyable, and rewarding; the professional and volunteer staff members strive to set an example, give support to the patients, and help them master new situations.

Our seven-day camping trip was really an extension of our regular field trips. The plan had been developed gradually by the patient-staff group, and serious planning and anticipation had continued for several weeks. Each patient agreed to pay part of his expenses. The patients saw the prospective camping trip primarily as an outing or recreational activity, something like a vacation. The staff viewed it as a therapeutic experiment, a more formidable challenge to patients' adaptive capacities, and a significant event in the lives of the patients, something they could strive for and then remember as an accomplishment.

Because of the day status of the patients, voluntary participation in the camping trip seemed to arouse more ambivalence than would be noted in hospital patients. To hospital patients, a camping trip may appear as a release from the ordered and regimented hospital life, but to our day-center patients, the trip represented a return to a 24-hour program, with the prospects of increased regimentation and closer contact with other patients and staff. These anxieties probably accounted for the marked indecision that we observed. Initially about thirty of the day-center members expressed their intention to go. Two weeks before departure, however, only seven were still willing. At that point the staff began active efforts to sell the trip, resolve problems and doubts, and allay conflicts. The patients offered various rationalizations and unconvincing excuses; a patient who had been unemployed for eight years claimed he had the prospect of a job that very week. A series of group-therapy and role-playing sessions that were focused on anxieties and problems related to the trip seemed to help. Gradually the number of patients planning to go rose to twenty-five, but even on the day of departure one patient arrived in a business suit, carrying his suitcase, and announced that he was not going. His suitcase was loaded on the bus and he was asked to accompany it, which he did. He subsequently adjusted very well and seemed to benefit from the experience.

By the hour of departure, enthusiasm was high. It lasted the first few hours and through the picnic lunch. On the road, however, the enthusiasm gradually dwindled, and by the time the long bus trip was over, the patients seemed subdued and worried. When we arrived at the ranch entrance, we found that the bus was unable to travel all the way to the camp site because of the steep roadway and the need to travel part way on the river bottom. The group was unloaded and transported the rest of the way in pickup trucks. At the start of the unloading the patients, judging from their comments, felt abandoned and trapped beyond the point of return. However, the unexpected development seemed to be an icebreaker. The *abandonment,* followed by *rescue* when we reached the camp site, restored the jolly, adventurous mood, which lasted until bedtime.

The camp arrangements were almost ideal. We had the use of one camping area on a 2000-acre ranch located on the Frio River, in rocky, hilly, peaceful surroundings. The patients and staff members (seven professionals and five volunteers) shared quarters, meals, activities, and all work assignments. This democratic arrangement seemed to facilitate communication, closer knowledge of one another as people, and closer observation of patients' reactions to this new environment. Several patients said that staff members for the first time seemed to be real people. Staff members found that they developed a much fuller understanding of the patients, even those with whom they had worked daily for many months.

One of the first things to arouse general interest was the chance to observe wild animals. This area has many small birds, wild turkeys, deer, goats, squirrels, and other small animals. On the morning after arrival, one patient spotted a goat that appeared to be stranded on a cliff ledge. The goat became the focus of general concern for several hours, and it was suggested that its apparent plight symbolized the trapped feelings of the patients. The goat got off safely, of course, giving the incident a happy ending.

The daily schedule consisted of a number of structured activities: painting, crafts, dancing, organized hikes, swimming, and campfire sessions. There were also many informal activities, such as fishing, cards and other games, short informal hikes, and nature study. The assigned daily chores, especially preparing and serving meals and the KP work, took part of each day. Meals became very important to everyone, and they were one of the best times for general socializing.

Many of the patients spent a lot of time doing nothing, just loafing and relaxing. We noticed that, especially during the first few days, several of the patients appeared to use sleep as a defense mechanism. However, the group's enthusiasm tended to involve everyone in the more organized activities.

Initially there was a noticeable contrast between the attitudes of most of the patients and those of the staff. The staff members were savoring each new experience, seeking new adventures, and attempting to prolong each day. Most of the patients seemed to be trying to get through each new activity without any emotional crisis or difficulty; at the end of the day they would almost rush to bed to forestall any further demands or problems. As the week went by, however, they appeared to become more adventurous and more like the staff members in their attitudes.

Several events were high points. One was the sighting of the Echo satellite as it passed overhead; in these remote, isolated, natural surroundings, this evidence of scientific achievement was particularly impressive. On Sunday morning a brief religious service was held, and in this setting it was unusually moving. During the week we held an art contest, a beard-growing contest, a bridge tournament, and a bingo night. One of the most successful events was a long hike led by the director of the ranch. He pointed out many of the natural resources, talked about Indian lore, and told stories of the history of the area. One evening he attended a bonfire session and told local stories and legends. The patients were drawn to the ranch director, partly because he was an interesting person but also because he was seen as a link to the outside world.

Several critical incidents occurred without disrupting the week in any major way. A woman patient and a man staff member turned over in a canoe. One patient was stung by a scorpion. A woman patient had a vivid hallucination one night, causing some stir in her cabin; however, the other occupants were able to reassure her.

As the end of the week approached, several of the patients began to talk of leaving prematurely. Again we noted a certain degree of ambivalence; for instance, the patient who talked the most about leaving never shaved his beard and later won the beard-growing contest. No patient took any concrete steps to leave, and by the end of the week almost all of them expressed their reluctance to return home.

How did the camping experience affect the condition and behavior of the patients? The immediate effects, as judged by direct observation and by the diaries kept by all patients, were almost all positive. As the days in camp passed, the patients showed increased appetites, fewer sleep disturbances, fewer physical complaints, more feeling, and even some improvements in posture, gait, and gracefulness. A few seemed unable to relax and let themselves participate freely and spontaneously. These individuals appeared to be trying to get by. However, after safely returning home they also spoke of that experience as one that they would like to repeat. No patient in our group of twenty-five became worse as the result of the week of camping.

After we returned, attendance at the day center sharply increased. Patients who went on the trip often mentioned it with enthusiasm, and those who did not go expressed regret. We think that there may be lasting gains in the living habits of the patients involved; they experienced a whole range of new activities, responsibilities, relationships, and situations, and they successfully handled almost all of them. Future ventures should be easier for this rigid and retiring group.

Is therapeutic camping compatible with a day center program and caseload? In our opinion it is, perhaps once a year. Such a special annual trip might give direction to many of the year-round activities. We also believe that more frequent camping excursions could be usefully worked into the program if we could limit them to overnight or weekend trips to camping areas located closer to Houston.

CHAPTER X

PROGRAM THEMES AT A PSYCHIATRIC DAY CAMP

Ruth G. Whittekin

Surely mental illness is the loneliest disease. At its onset, communicating becomes difficult with friends and family, and impossible with strangers. We have men who have lived on the same ward for years who do not know each other by name.

After working for some time with a group of chronic, regressed schizophrenic men, I began looking for some new experiences for them. I wanted the experiences to be so different from drab hospital routine that they might generate some new awareness in these long-term patients. I have found that, in order to attract patients from behind their schizophrenic barriers, activities need to be planned and executed with imagination. Music should be lively, colors bright, and materials and games varied and interesting.

Keeping those qualities in mind, I planned a five-day *camp by day* program. On Monday, Tuesday, and Wednesday the patients would leave the hospital by bus at 8:30 A.M. to go to a camp site and would return at 3:30 P.M. On Thursday the day would begin at 6:30 A.M. and end at 1:30 P.M. and on Friday our bus would leave at 1:30 P.M. and return at 8:30 P.M. That schedule would give the campers the experience of having all three meals out of doors. The theme chosen for the day camp was an *Indian powwow.*

To carry out the program, I needed much help from other disciplines, and the program became a joint project of the dietetics, occupational therapy, and recreational therapy departments. Several weeks of planning and of obtaining approvals followed. The ward physician and head nurse of the building in which the men lived contributed much time and effort to the over-all planning. Our camp staff consisted of a dietitian and her helper, an occupational therapist, a licensed vocational (practical) nurse, a psychiatric aide, two women volunteers, and myself. The personnel of the entire building acted as back-up staff.

Our first task was to select twenty-four men we felt would benefit from camping. One or two prospects had to be eliminated because they were on modified diets, which could not be easily provided at the camp. Our final list included a group of long-term regressed schizophrenic patients, the youngest of whom was thirty-eight and the oldest seventy.

To prepare the men for the project, we held three preliminary meetings to discuss some of the plans for camp without giving away any of the surprises. The Indian powwow idea seemed to be an excellent tool for penetrating the schizophrenic wall. Each of the four staff leaders was assigned five men, and four men were to assist me in coordinating the activities of the other groups. My group became the Huaco tribe, hosts to the Cheyenne, Cherokee, Sioux, and Kickapoo. We believed that being part of a small group would give each man a feeling of acceptance and belonging. He would have an opportunity to excel in various competitive games for his own glory as well as to earn points for his tribe.

The dietitian encouraged the patients to help plan menus. Food was especially important for these men, because many of them were very poor eaters. The occupational therapist put the men to work painting boxes for supplies, converting coffee cans into individual camp stoves, and making award plaques and a camp scrapbook. One group made a reflector oven for baking biscuits and cakes. The occupational therapist also laid plans for craft activities at camp: weaving Johnson grass into place mats; implanting sticks, stones, and grass in plaster of Paris to make attractive wall plaques; and placing candles in old tin cans to serve as hand lanterns.

From the first day at camp, the enthusiasm with which everyone tackled the demanding schedule was quite rewarding. On Monday, Tuesday, and Wednesday the first thirty minutes was given to such tasks as making coffee, cleaning tables, cleaning latrines, and collecting and cutting wood for cooking. That was followed by a thirty-minute coffee break. Everyone looked forward to the surprise sweets the dietitian brought each day to go with the coffee.

Immediately after the coffee break the tribes began such activities as cooking lunch, forming scouting parties, going fishing, working at nature crafts, and devising original games for the afternoon council ring. All work stopped at 11:30 A.M. for lunch, followed by clean-up and a period of relaxation. It was gratifying to see how the poor appetites of some patients improved in a short time.

Promptly at 1 P.M. the tribes resumed activities, which were changed often to maintain the men's interest. One hour before returning to the hospital, all tribes assembled in the giant council ring for competitive games. Each tribe presented original games, and all joined in other games adapted by the host tribe. By the time of the first council ring, each tribe had made head bands for its members, which they wore with pride every day.

Each day was more successful than the last. Men who at first had not been enthusiastic kept asking, "What time do we go tomorrow?" On Thursday, the day we were to leave at 6:30 A.M., one patient who had had to be coaxed to attend camp got up at 4 A.M. to see if it was time to get ready.

The breakfast cook-out on Thursday was a new experience for all participants; each man cooked bacon and an egg on his own tin-can stove. That fare was supplemented by food cooked over the main campfire, because appetites were ravenous. On Friday we held an evening campfire. Each man had voted to buy his own steak to broil at the final meal; in that way he had a feeling of sharing the expense of camp.

After supper all the tribes assembled at the council ring for the awards program. An award plaque was presented to the Kickapoo as the tribe who had won the most points during the week. The outstanding camper in each tribe was given a canteen book and was invited to go to the next camp as part of the staff. We also gave special awards for outstanding contributions to the operation of the camp.

In a ceremony around the campfire, the award-winning campers and leaders were made honorary members of the host tribe, the Huaco. At that time the host tribe presented the completed scrapbook of all the camp activities, and the tribal leaders sang a song they had written about the camp and the staff. Then to the surprise of almost everyone, a local Scout troop arrived dressed in Indian costumes. Everyone agreed that their authentic Indian dances around the campfire were a fitting climax to a great week.

We have subsequently held two additional camps, with the themes of a cowboy roundup and a five-day imaginary tour of Old Mexico. All have been so successful that we are convinced of the therapeutic value of such a program. How do you measure its success? Happy faces, enthusiasm, increased appetites, experiences to describe to others, and greater acceptance of reality are among the signs, and we observed them frequently among all our camping groups.

CHAPTER XI

CAMPS AS MENTAL HEALTH INSTITUTIONS

ERNEST HARMS

THIS TOPIC represents a field in which the author has an intense personal interest. This interest surpasses any objective conviction of the unusual importance of the problem of summer recreation in the life of our youth and the various mental health aspects connected with it. From earliest youth the author received the major part of his education and enjoyment from the Continental fresh air movement and during almost all his later life he has been active in some form of open air living. He became even more closely identified with summer camps when, at the end of the last decade, he was asked by a governmental agency to survey the present main features of the American private camp and to make suggestions for the improvement of the unduly commercialized conditions by administrative measures. From this survey grew the idea of an experimental camp of his own, an idea to which Elizabeth McK. Scott and Robert C. Scott lent their enthusiastic cooperation, and which resulted in the founding of the Broadview Farm Camps. These are now in their fourth year of operation and so nearly approaching completion that in a year or two they may be presented to the camping world as a new type of recreational institution.

The author feels that he should mention the above facts because out of them grew his interest in the mental hygiene problem of the summer camp. Actually it not only grew from these experiences, it was forced upon him with the overwhelming force of an almost tragic reality.

In introducing this topic I hope our readers will not expect me to repeat the apparently indispensable quotation for every American book on camping: "What President Elliot said." I hope I am also excused from telling how American psychologists discovered Camp Ahmek and there found the most attractive object for their test-mill. We know that the inner motivation of the American camping movement is deeper and more serious than can be indicated by the behavior testing of American psychologists of twenty years ago; and we must say that the wave of camping literature created under the auspices of the applied psychologists has done more to divert the original camping impulse into a blind alley than to give it real encouragement. Unfortunately it cannot be said that the camping movement returned to its original direction when the wave of psychologically inspired writing died away in the years before the start of World War II. On the contrary it reached new heights of commercialism.

There is no doubt that the study of human mental life, whether we call it psychology, characterology, mental hygiene, or anything else, is an important part of the effective arrangement of our camping aims. And that it is more important than knowledge of camp sites, or of sanitary and aquatic arrangements. However, we must not gain this attitude knowledge of camping from schematic results and from text books and investigations made in cities, but from original work in rural and camp settings. It must be—as I have called it earlier *camp-centered.* Any application of outside psychology will for the most part be valueless and even dangerous. Among the few recent camping publications there has been an almost paradoxical example, so paradoxical and dangerous that I feel impelled to point it out. A writer for the publishing enterprise of our largest youth educational body has issued a booklet with suggestions for good camping in which he felt that for once he should step aside from the test psychologist's viewpoint to that of modern analytical psychology in regard to camp work. For reasons I prefer not to discuss here, he conceived the idea of popularizing Carl Gustav Jung's dualistic attitude pattern of extravert and introvert. However, without real sincerity and probably without even the ability to understand and apply Jung's psychology, he has given an explanation and directions for applying these two terms which represent an actual danger, to the reader psychologically a serious one.

If we take the relationship of psychology and camping seriously, we must admit that the first period of this relationship was wrong and almost tragic, and that only lately have we become aware not only of the existence of a real psychology of camping but of its vital importance. We stand at the beginning of the development of a real camping psychology. This new and real psychology does not grow from the physical, nor even the mental camping need, from sleeping facilities and menus to ball playing, hiking, swimming or making friends, being a good counselor or a good camper, things that were outstanding in early camp psychology. It has been developed along other lines and quite empirically, based on the *troubles* of even a fairly normal child coming from a city environment, parental protection and overprotection into the quite different social environment of a camp in the woods or on a mountain top. This real and empiric camp psychology does not deal primarily with normal and simple attitudes but with those which cause difficulties and therefore it is to some extent an abnormal psychology. It follows the course of the whole history of the science of psychology. Starting out as a natural science, the psychiatrists, forced by tragic experience with the mentally sick, turned psychology into a mental science. To a certain extent the early camping psychology, with its application of test sheets and competition and *good camping marks* was a *psychology without a camper,* just as the early psychology was *a psychology without a psyche.* We learn now for the first time to deal with the real child and see all the psychological problems which arise on all sides. These problems are not those of normality but of abnormality and of adjustment needs, to say nothing of the mental hygiene aspects which also have a regulatory character. Of course, above and beyond this, is a real social and individual psychology of camp living with a different aspect from that presented in early books. But many years, probably a whole decade, must elapse before we are sufficiently mature and experienced to realize and produce such a camping psychology.

On this topic, I believe for the first time, an attempt is made to observe camping problems without the aid of colored glasses and with a sober realization of the task to be accomplished. Although these pages by leading workers in the field provide only a tentative approach, this seemed to be the only form in which the entire task could be made impressive to the mass of camp workers. I hope this will lead to intensive work in the field to which I am only too anxious to give any help which may be needed or desired. One of the first and most basic tasks will be to build the foundations of a really sound camp psychology by overcoming the ideological opinion carefully fostered by many camp directors and especially in organized groups such as the Boy Scouts and Campfire Girls. This takes for its ideal the perfectly normal child in the camp, an ideal that does not exist. There are adjustment problems to be solved with every child even if these problems may not be those of definitely abnormal behavior. The oversimplified and almost primitive camping philosophy must be superseded if we hope to make of camp and outdoor life the mental and physical recreational factor it must be in order to balance the frustrations and inversions suffered by youth in our cities.*

---

* An excellent essay on private camps today can be found in the April 1973 *Saturday Review of Education.*

CHAPTER XII

PSYCHOPATHOLOGIC RISKS OF CAMP LIFE

FRITZ REDL

NO, I AM NOT debunking camping at all. On the contrary, just because I am so firmly convinced of the tremendous value of camping, educationally and also as a means of therapy, I can afford to discuss a topic like this without fear of being misunderstood.

This is what I mean. We are using camping on various levels to help youngsters grow up. We use the camp for character training, for supportive mental hygiene, for the treatment of disturbed children, and for stimulation of normal values. But camping, being such a powerful drug, also shares the properties of all other powerful drugs on the market. It is risky, if the wrong person swallows it, or if the right one swallows too much of it, or if it is swallowed at the wrong time. In short, the camp itself is not only something through which children are supposed to adjust better, but also something to which they have to adjust.

This adjustment to camp life, which we take so much for granted, is not always easy, and sometimes the conflicts produced by the need for this adjustment outbalances the values to be derived from its accomplishment. For the city child especially, large scale group life far away from his home, exposure to nature in the raw without the protective comforts of the mechanized urban environment, can sometimes be quite a problem.

In most cases these difficulties can be counteracted, handled, adequately met; and we want to be sure that we meet them.

The following, therefore, is an attempt to analyze camp life in terms of its psychopathologic risks for those who have trouble making an adjustment to the medium.

The word *psychopathologic* refers only to camp life, not to the camper. I am not talking, here, about the problem child, but about the average normal youngster who is exposed to this new medium for the first time. If I list here the *psychopathologic risks* of camping, then this limitation is due to the nature of the topic. I could write a much longer and more impressive list of the values of camping and have done so in other places.

THE SNAKE IN THE GRASS, OR NATURE IN THE RAW

The enthusiastic books on nature and its effect on our soul have all been written by people who have attained an appreciation of values which not everybody starts out with. Nature is all that people say in their books and more. However, it includes much that they do not mention in their books. Let us remember the change from the overprotected city world, which constitutes the first exposure to camp life for a city child. The firmly built apartment house or suburban mansion is replaced by rustic log cabins or flimsy tents. And even the shack of the slum area child at least stands among other shacks in familiar urban environment, and therefore suggests much more security than the camp cabin. The toilet smells and the things that are supposed to prevent it from doing so, smell worse. Animals and insects such as spiders, flies, ants, intrude upon your privacy at a moment when the study of nature is not necessarily your main concern. That shady tree over there looks just like the one in that story book, under which the hero used to spin his daydreams. However; you have hardly sat down under it when it seems as if half your zoology textbook is set loose on you. At night it gets dark; you never noticed darkness so much, especially darkness that is filled with a variety of entirely unfamiliar sounds. Sometimes you hear a wild racket way up in the skies, just like in some of those murder movies or thriller-radio plays. A storm is fascinating to watch, but you also have to listen to it and maybe you have to step out into it to get to the washhouse or dining hall. There is an absence of all familiar noises like the street car, the automobiles on that drive behind your house, and the street vendor. Maybe most of those noises are less loud and nervewracking; but they are certainly more frightening, for you have trouble in identifying most of them and the stillness of a nonmechanized world brings them out more threateningly.

City children have heard and read about storms, animals, nature, and have used these images as props in their nightmares and daydreams. What isolated contacts they have made with nature usually were in broad daylight or in the protective custody of father or mother on that car trip. Suddenly all nature is let loose on that child from town. It stirs up most of the half forgotten childhood anxieties. Fantasy fears and real discomfort are mixed into a frightening blend. The result is that many children are frightened at camp much of the time. They may have to handle more anxieties in the first few camp days than during the entire school year; and anxieties, for the management of which, routine, experience, and protective understanding have not been adequately developed.

The symptomology of these anxieties is fascinating to watch. Few of them come out into the open in their direct form, recognizable for what they are. The majority of them suffer the destiny of *displacement* before they can be expressed. They assume all sorts of disguises: dissatisfaction with the cook, complaints of lack of cleanliness, opposition to the program, and antagonism to the cabin. A heavier disguise, the safest they can assume is that of transformation into the opposite. Johnny's neurotic fear of "nature in the raw" is shown to you as an unreasonable bravado attitude against all health and safety rules; his fear of the snake in the grass may be turned into a compulsive display of what looks like "nature study interest."

The basic meaning of all this, however, is obvious and can be summed up in a simple statement: Johnny is exposed to a revival of some old childhood neurosis, or he is exposed to a new one in the making. In both cases he needs considerable help from you before the camp can really take hold.

PARENTS THROUGH THE SCREEN PORCH

For many children the first camp experience also means the first more decisive separation from the familiar life at home. This is, of course, true for those with a somewhat overprotective but very happy family life, but it is just as true for those whose home and family life is really confused and unhappy. Even if the home environment is less pleasant than camp, it is certainly more familiar, and adaptive mechanisms to cope with its discomforts are well developed. Separation from home, parents—even a temporary voluntary, well planned, and on the whole desirable one—cuts deep into the unconscious layers of Johnny's or Mary's case history. Some children love camp and enjoy every moment of it; but they know that mother would really be quite disappointed to realize that Junior is so independent of her. This joy of camp life is, then, tinged with guilt feelings in terms of early childhood loyalties. Other children go through feelings of discomfort at camp which they might be able to handle under their own steam. They know, however, that their parents really want them away and this additional sting produces a conflict beyond their power to allay. Others again move through a happy phase of emancipation from home and enjoy their newly found independence for a while. With the next letter or package, or a letter and package of the cabin mate, the whole world of childhood conflict suddenly rises before their eyes; the camp and whatever it tries to do may be engulfed. Some children enjoy the chance to unpack all the negative feelings they had piled up against family and home routine and to throw it rebelliously at the camp-substitutes, indulging in a pleasurable fight against the windmills of their case history. Others withdraw from the threat of adjustment to camp into a glorified nostalgic daydream about home, painting the picture with colors it never possessed, are in for a rude awakening on the first visiting day. . . . In short, parents and home look different if you look at them through the porch screen of the camp veranda. This experience of a different feeling about home and the home folks is an upsetting experience for many youngsters to go through, even where the outcome is to the good.

The symptoms of this phenomenon are varied. It is caught most concisely in the letters the children write and the stories the children tell about camp. Most of them have little to do with the emotional and culinary reality of camp life. Most of them are designed to hit the consumer in a spot where it either pleases or hurts, to glorify some and to cover up other phases of real camp life. Camp directors would be horrified if they knew how often Johnny has to tell Mama he loves her by making the camp counselor out to be a torturing sadist and the camp director a parsimonious exploiter of little children's stomachs. Parents would be horrified if they knew how often that glorified description of the marvelous canoe trip really means an accusation against their own role in life with Johnny at home. With skillful planning, with good luck in the choice of camp counselors, and with unusual wisdom in the handling of moments of depression as well as of rebellion, Johnny and Mary will cope with this new experience in their life. If the camp is less skilled, the home background just a few notches more confused or really wrong, this *adjustment phase* in the children's life may in itself become the source of a neurotic development. Its proper handling is one of the things you hope for when you send Johnny to camp.

EGO-IDEALS FOR RENT

Most of us who invite children to come to our camps have a deep-seated ambition to provide an especially *valuable experience* for them, to produce some changes or improvements in their character traits, value sensitivities or at least in their ability to bow in the right way before the altar of Emily Post. The camps which can claim serious consideration educationally, certainly aim to make somewhat of a "new person" out of Johnny, and if they succeed are proud of the way in which "he had taken to camp life." The *ego ideal* of the *Good Camper* has, as far as I know, not yet been studied by sociologists and anthropologists and I certainly recommend it to them for study. I dare not bring up all the amazing things we would discover in such a study but I should like to say this much: The ego ideal of the good camper is a special ethical standard developed in American society. Parts of it are derived from cultures which we conquered and exterminated (consider the heavy emphasis on Indian lore), other parts are nostalgic reminiscences of a world which our nation has left behind (the lumberman at the campfire, the conqueror of mountains and streams, the skillful survivor against odds through crafty use of ax and bow and arrow). Some parts of this ego ideal are, of course, colored by the personal idiosyncrasies of the camp director or the people who give the money to run the camp (the different shades of religious philosophy, the varying styles of group life from autocratic militarism through various forms of cultist groups of "friendship for friendships' sake"). Some of the components of this camper ideal come from social pressures (a chance to teach Mary how to eat with fork and knife) and some from a simple urge to have the children stored during the summer vacation without too much damage risk (the stress of being *good,* constructive, adult-acceptable at all times).

For our purpose it is sufficient to remind ourselves that the exposure to this new ego ideal of the good camper, in whatever form Johnny may meet it at any particular time, is a temporary one only. This personality ideal is not for sale, it is only for rent. Camp and the style of life to which you want Johnny to adjust, runs only for a few weeks. The style of life to which Johnny will have to return, will vary to a considerable degree from this personality image of the good camper which you support with so much campfire glow. This temporary rental of special ideals, parts of which we want to be incorporated for good, part of which we want Johnny to discard as soon as the camp train hits the city terminal, may sometimes constitute a problem of its own. Let me mention only a few from among the rich variety of pathologic problems encountered along this line: If Johnny has too much trouble in adopting this ego ideal of the good camper for summer use, he will be a misfit in camp. He is doomed to be the scapegoat for the others, will be looked down upon by the camp adults (no matter what a genius he may be in his urban life) and all he can do is sit in the corner and either cry, pout, or spin megalomanic daydreams against the group. If Johnny is too enthusiastic in becoming that 100 percent good camper, he may sometimes bite off more than he can chew and end by becoming a failure in his own eyes; or he may really assume temporarily a tremendous amount of fame and leadership, but on a basis on which it will not be granted to him when he gets back to his hometown. He may push himself into a nostalgic ego ideal of woodsmanship and pioneerdom for which there is little use after his return to *civilian life,* for only people who want to become camp directors themselves in their later life, and a very few other exceptions, can afford to turn into cultists of nature and permanent camp fire enthusiasts. As for Johnny or Mary, we do not want them to swap their identification with the complexity of urban occupations for these dated daydreams; we only want them to use some of the trappings of these ego ideals during the rental period for the inculcation of some of the values smuggled in under their romantic disguise.

It is interesting to discover that many very good city children, do not make *easy campers* on that score, nor do some of the very bad ones. For them the new imagery of a mixture of woodsman, pioneer and Indian warrior culture is either strange, funny, or frightening. Instead of feeling secure and happy with us, they feel strange, lost, and out of place. The semi-religious ritual which the American camping movement has developed for the cultivation of this ego ideal as a substitute for a genuine youth cult, is often rejected vehemently at the first exposure to camp. Some of the children who take too easily to these ideals, the so called *natural campers,* are sometimes prone to exploit them for pathological use. Instead of being inspired by them, they smuggle their ego ideals home for permanent exploitation in terms of an easy superiority of the nature cultist against more realistic forms of city life, and hide their inability to adjust to a more complex structure of life behind the glorified and simple concepts of a romantic escapist cult. The camps will do well to keep this phase of their life and work well in mind. Sometimes our diet is too poor in terms of ego ideals, sometimes too rich with them. Sometimes we do too superficial a job of rental, sometimes we try too hard to make permanent what is meant for use in summertime only. Sometimes we confuse the ritual form and the basic character content, and sometimes we fall so in love with our own ego ideals that we forget to study the consumer who is going to use them.

The resistance to, or enthusiasm for these ego ideals sometimes produce a phase of conflict and confusion in our campers. To classify our stock of ego ideals, to help the youngsters who are confused about them, is an important phase of camp policy.

CAN YOU HOWL WITH THE WOLVES?

One of the great values of camping for many youngsters is that it shifts the emphasis from the adjustment of one child to the dominating adult pattern of life, toward the task of adjustment to life with a group of other children his own age. This ambition to be a good member of a youthful group and to make a go of it even in the light of conflict and discomfort, is a frequent theme of camp life. On the other hand, we should not forget that this very shift in developmental emphasis from *Life with Father* to *Life with your peers* is sometimes a difficult and painful one, and that not all children are ready for it at the same time. In fact, this very desire to be popular with the rest of the gang is often in direct conflict with old, deeply ingrained demands of parental obedience. Many children are, through the philosophy of camping, often thrown into a temporary conflict between their ideal of being a *regular guy* with the group and their childhood concepts of what constitutes the earmarks of a *good little boy.* I have, in my own camps, often seen a child who is suddenly confronted by such problems. Johnny was, for instance, always so proud of being a good little boy, and definitely not like *some other kids in his neighborhood* who didn't behave so well in school. Suddenly his father discovers that he is too *good* for his own taste, and wants him *toughened up* a little. The camp is supposed to do the job. Result: Johnny finds himself in a group of somewhat more emancipated boys, some of whom with what he would consider a daredevil philosophy of life. Instead of imitating them, their behavior scares him stiff; each independent act of the more sophisticated or more independent youngsters stirs up old guilt feelings in Johnny's father-identified soul. The result may be any of the following: fear of the other children whom he considers *bad;* wild imitation (overdoing it) of the worst of them, so as not to be considered a sissy; or indefinable feelings of confusion, irritation, anxiety attacks, lack of sleep, loss of appetite, and a vague feeling of homesickness with crying spells. In short, in order to live in a pack, a child has to learn to howl with the wolves. What if he is afraid of them; if he doesn't want to be considered a wolf at that time, or he knows his parents really wouldn't like this howl if they heard it? The over-protected child is the most frequent victim of this type of conflict. There is something like a vicious circle at work in his case. The parents sent him to camp because they knew he was over-protected. His very over-protection makes it hard for him to react without anxiety or guilt to the group life at camp. If he does get over this, the hangovers from his over-protected superego development make him feel nervous and guilty for the very accomplishment of the emancipation for which he was sent to camp.

Typical expressions of this problem are fear of other children, greed for popularity, extreme shyness, extreme clowning, unreasonable rebellion against even reasonable adults under the guise of pack-loyalty, or open symptoms of neurotic fear and anxiety directly in relation to the group or in displaced forms. The most frequent of those are extreme forms of competitive pride, a mania for collecting prizes and badges as a cover for a lack of real adjustment to the things that count.

THE LONELINESS OF GROUP LIFE

People who are enthusiastic about something are liable to talk themselves into such enthusiasm about the particular form of salvation they preach that they soon begin to think it is the only one. Thus, they tend to oversell a good thing, to pretend that the particular value they happen to sell is the only thing that counts, and forget about all the other ingredients which go into a well balanced and healthy diet. In a democracy, with its strong belief in group life, it is only natural that the camping movement may sometimes fall into that mistake. For group life is the strongest medicine we camp people have to offer, and the uniqueness of the camp form of group life is our natural domain.

I have seen well planned group life do wonders for children, but not everybody can stand equally much of it. Some children are suddenly exposed to group life before they are ready for it. Even if there was too little chance for group play in Johnny's life at home, that does not mean he should have nothing else from now on. Like all good things, even good group life has its drawbacks and limitations, and people need sometimes a vacation from it. First, group life is hard on one's standards of individual comfort. Especially for twenty-four hours a day. Johnny is not anti-social, just because he would rather take a shower or urinate by himself. Mary is not an isolate just because she hates interrupting her morning daydream in favor of a flag raising ritual. As to arts and crafts—let us not forget that none of the great symphonies were composed by a committee, and that few great books have been written by people while they were dancing "turkey in the straw." While we often do a good job by offering chances for creative group life, we sometimes undernourish our customers in terms of opportunities for privacy and freedom from group exposure. Children need not only to learn how to be with a group and how to accept group pressures, but also how and when to have the courage to be on their own, and to defend themselves against the pressures of group and mob psychology. The result is, that some children begin to overindulge in the delicacies of group life; some vomit them even before they can be enjoyed. Some go through the motions of group adjustment, but feel horribly alone underneath. The necessity of adjusting themselves to so many people so much of the time makes it difficult for some children to make any deeper adjustments to a few. The threat of having to share friends, adults and other children, with so many, or to be exposed to the constant danger of rivalry, makes it hard for some children to dare to make any deep relationships at all. While the group gives the numerical opportunity for many friendships, it often mars the psychological chance for all of them. I do not say that the group necessarily has this effect, but I do maintain that I have seen it happen, and this in itself we should recognize as an important pathological risk. I have seen children *opened up* for the enjoyment of group life through a summer's camp experience. I also have seen children acquire a deep hatred for all group life through one summer's experience. So we had better remember how important it is for us to figure out which way we can swing them. Skillful programming, and group psychological antisepsis in the choice of leadership techniques are the best safeguards against this risk.

WHAT CAN WE DO ABOUT ALL THIS?

My list of psychopathological risks of camp life is not only incomplete, but it is barely a scratch on the surface. In addition, I have restricted myself to selecting a few illustrations out of the field of *individual hazards*. There is an even wider area of pathological risks of camp life, which I have not even mentioned, the psychopathology of group life. Instead of expanding into that field, I had best make a few remarks on the question of what we can do about pathological risks.

Of course, there is no specific answer to a general question. Real help can be given to the parent, camp director or the child only on the basis of a specific analysis of Johnny and his present development, and of a situational analysis of the troublesome incidents in camp life. I think, however, a few general suggestions could be offered even in as short a statement as this one.

1. Avoid Multiple Shock

Many children can stand adjustment to one or two new and difficult items at a time. Before you send them to camp, figure out just which phase of camp life is liable to be traumatic for them. Some will enjoy life with nature, but adjusting to a gang of strange children will be hard for them. Others will like everything, except they have never been away from mother before. Others, again, will like the company, but the athletic angle of outdoor life is going to be quite a shock, and they will worry if anybody finds out they wet the bed. . . .

Make your selection strategically. Pick the camp that promises most understanding and help in the area where Johnny's contact with camp life is liable to be the most difficult.

Do not send them, if you expect more than two essential aspects of camp life to be traumatic. For instance, do not send Johnny if he is scared of the dark and also of the other children and also has never lived away from home before. Or if you do, send him to a camp which promises unusually skillful and professional handling of most of these problems.

2. *Psychiatry for the Uninterested*

Camps, with few exceptions, are frightened of anything that even approaches Psychiatry or Mental Hygiene. In some, this is because of the personal idiosyncracies of the camp directors or sponsors. Others would like psychiatric help, but they are afraid of what the parents would say if they knew. In short it is difficult for psychiatric knowledge to infiltrate the field of normal camping with normal children where it is needed most. I am trying to point out that if you want to avoid the psychopathological risk for your normal children, you have to train your staff so that they are aware of what they are supposed to detect and avoid. You need special consultants who can warn you of the risk areas of your clientele, and you need good in-service training of your staff so that they can discover and handle whatever pathological risks they unearth.

3. *The Miracle of Grouping*

Many children have trouble with their first camp adjustment. Whether they can handle this trouble or not, often depends less on them than on the group to which they were assigned. For instance, Johnny is not quite ready to howl with the wolves. The question arises as to how loud do his co-wolves howl. If Johnny is exposed to a group of boys who are just slightly more athletic than he, but in their personal behavior violate none of his individual value standards too badly, he will be all right in a few days. But if he is placed in a group where some of the boys have the precocity of a young adolescent while he is barely emerging from the phase of *young child,* you have an insoluble problem on your hands. The skill of antiseptic grouping is an involved one; I am fascinated by the increased interest the public and private camping field has shown in this aspect, but I am equally impressed with the paucity of organized and usable research available.

4. *The Importance of Timing*

Many parents confuse the question of what a child should become eventually, with what he is able to take right now. Thus, they may say that Johnny *needs* a camp experience. What they mean is usually: "I saw a good camper the other day; I wish my boy would show more of that attitude than he does now." The question of the period of his development at which he is ready for camp experience to take effect, is an entirely different one. A badly timed camp experience, even though the camp itself was superb, may do more harm than good. And in such a case, the camp is not to blame.

5. *Program and the Human Equation*

Program and routine are really only frozen forms of human relationships. There is no such thing as a *good* program or *good* discipline as such. Your pathological risks are lowest if there is a free flow between programming and disciplinary policies on the one hand, and the total atmosphere of human relations and your child, on the other. The amount of thought that goes into relating the two is the best safeguard against pathological risks.

6. *The Protective Coating of a Good Camp Atmosphere*

Some of the difficult experiences Johnny or Mary meet during their first camp exposure are not as traumatic as they might be, provided the total atmosphere of the camp is one of happy personal relationships. In a camp where Johnny feels at ease with the adults, his fear of other children, his worry about the threats of nature, and his difficulty in making a success of his role in the group, will not upset him too much. Even if it does, he will show this in one way or another and give you a chance to observe it; or he will go to you with some vague complaints which you will have no trouble in relating to the real issue. And you need not be afraid, either, that Johnny will not *know* how helpful you can be to him. Children have an astounding intuition into this very factor of human emotions and are much better at sensing it than we are in figuring it out and putting it into scientific terms.

CHAPTER XIII

UNREGIMENTED CAMPS FOR PROBLEM CHILDREN

LOIS GOODRICH

CITIES ARE perilous places. A person can live and die in an apartment house and never be known by those who live in the same house. This is not a good place for children to discover the foundations of life. The city is materialistic and the struggle for material things tends to dwarf the developmental potentialities. The city is a place of crowds; crowds are terrible dangers. When crowd psychology works, the primitive emerges and people behave at primitive levels. Cities are rootless because they are far from the soil. Lack of soil and lack of space are perils to family life. The individual feels he does not have family rootage. This is actuated by crowds, anonymity and materialism, and the individual has to fight for the preservation of his sense of the significant.

Contrast this with camp which offers ideal opportunities for living together decently and kindly—relating ourselves to the outer world, to other people, to work which we can do and which needs us. Small wonder that campers write, as did this 17-year-old camper of several seasons:

> I cannot put my finger on the things camp means to me. I only know that whenever I see something lovely, whenever I feel the uplift of something fine and clean, these things are always associated in my thinking with camp experiences. Somewhere in the fun and the satisfaction of living together with other people outdoors, I found a sense of values, an understanding of the fundamental things that count, which I could not have found in any book or lecture. This, I think, is the deepest value of camping: it imparts a wisdom beyond knowledge, a sort of awareness of beauty and strength. . . . For the peace and the beauty of the lake, the strength and breadth

of the tree-covered hills, and the lasting security of many strong friendships, I am grateful for being a camper.

Unfortunately not every camp is so conceived as to bring about such effects on lives, but those where leaders have dared leave regimentation and rigid schedules behind and put campers on their own to meet and work out real life situations and problems (learning to live in small family groups in a back-to-the-earth simple life in the woods, of providing for food, shelter, and their own welfare and happiness) have the rare opportunity of discovering the real camper and of having that camper discover himself and his place in the community. The effects of such camping upon the average or even the disturbed city child has been worthy of note. It is with some of these effects as observed in the children sent to *Life Camp* (the camp with which the writer is most familiar) that this article will deal.

Let us look first at the life in such a camp and its possibilities for far-reaching effects. A family of eight children and two counselors live together twenty-four hours a day in a part of the woods all their own, in shelters they either build or care for, planning and preparing their own meals, building their stoves and tables, exploring and using their natural surroundings, planning and carrying out their own program of adventurous living.

Individual adjustment takes place here far more quickly than it does in the regimented camp program copied from school, where the children travel from group to group, counselor to counselor, at the sound of a bell. There, the shy one goes from place to place unnoticed and little changed when she boards the train for home. The loud, selfish one demands all the attention and the best equipment for crafts, sports, swimming, etc.; and though her demanding nature is surely annoying, no one counselor has her long enough to do anything more than sigh with relief when the gong sounds sending her to the next activity. The camper grouping in each activity is different, so that even group pressure has little effect on either the shy or the domineering. In this set-up, the camp could do little more than the school.

In a camp decentralized into small groups where the same eight children live together every day, all day, each child finds she is vital to the group: the shy and the selfish, the over-bearing.

In order that the group have breakfast, there must be wood-gatherers, fire-builders, cooks, table setters, dishwashers. By the end of the first day the group has discovered the leader, the poor sport, the lagging one, the attention-getter, etc., and the shy one has found she is important; the group is dependent upon her for her part of breakfast, and they can't go on with the exciting plans of the day until this responsibility has been carried well. There is no need for assignments or for artificial motivation for crafts when girls need a stove for meals, a rack to get a suitcase off the wet ground, a table from which to eat, or a bowl to hold an attractive flower arrangement for the birthday party or the arrival of guests. There is no limit to the range of creative opportunities in food, crafts, song, dance all growing out of the situation at hand.

A program is planned together by vote of the group. There is no place for selfishness to exist. Consideration for the wishes of others must prevail when the group is facing the difficulties and adventures of living in the woods in all weather. It is a program of putting people on their own to develop self-reliance and security in the realization of self and their own abilities, and of finding a place for that self in a group of people—balanced living as Christ meant it with His words: "He who would find his life must lose it. . . ." Add to this the quiet effect of the woods, the partnership with the world outdoors, in contrast to the impact of city mobs, and it is no wonder that psychiatrists write such letters to camp directors as:

> We feel that Marilyn has been tremendously helped by her camp experience and that it has been one of the major factors in helping her to a fairly good adjustment in the community in spite of the severely disturbed situation in her family.

Or, "Camp seems to be the one thing that gives Phyllis a sense of stability."

Let us look for a moment at unattractive Miriam, aged ten, with a very nervous mother who compares her unfavorably with the younger, attractive, five-year-old sister for whom Miriam must take almost total responsibility. The father is eccentric and gives the children no affection or companionship. The older sisters are emotionally isolated from the rest of the family and take no interest in Miriam. Mother buys Miriam's clothing from rummage sales. It is ill-fitting and she is large for her age, awkward and ungainly. She is intelligent, with good school marks, but has no belief in her own capacities—depreciates her own abilities and tears her clothing and gets very dirty when she is unhappiest. She has been beaten by groups of Negro girls in the neighborhood. She enters camp where she cries at the slightest criticism and has to be shown simple things such as how to put flour in a measuring cup. Her physical awkwardness is even more apparent, but she excels in dramatics and story telling and reads so well she is chosen to read the group's final ceremonial scroll. She begins to overcome fear of water and learns swimming strokes. She cries less and shows signs of self-confidence when she seeks companionship and is accepted slightly by one girl.

Her second summer she is more talkative and active. She is given praise at every turn. She is able to ask for suggestions about her clothing combinations and her hair arrangement. The girls begin to accept her into the group. She works harder in swimming, and the counselor chooses her to demonstrate the back float. She still is terribly awkward, dropping her food and falling over stones; she is growing fast physically.

Her third summer at camp she jokes with others but is not totally accepted. She excels when given encouragement. She stops running to counselors for help in group troubles, but is capable of facing them alone successfully.

In the fall, after her fourth season at camp, her mother writes as follows:

> My daughter, Miriam, was shy and reserved, kept to herself, had no friends. She used to get mixed up in fights and trouble. I was worried about her. Ever since her first summer in camp there was an improvement until now she is one of the most popular girls in her class at school and is asked to all their birthday parties, etc., is in the Christmas play, is taking dancing and piano lessons. I am very thankful to camp as I know they had a lot to do with the wonderful change in her.

Let us note briefly other parent responses:

> Not only can Irene do things for herself, but she wants to do things for herself. For instance she learned how to bake at camp.

> Now if she wants something and I am too busy, she will go right ahead and bake something whereas before she was afraid to do so.
>
> As for Zelda herself, I think the most important thing she has brought from camp is that she learned to mingle with people. Learned that life is a sort of give and take. (Zelda had no friends her entire *first* summer—but isolated herself with a book and the camp cat.)
>
> Imagine my surprise when Rose Ann, previously a timid child, returned almost an extrovert. You cannot estimate my delight when I tell you that she has maintained this desirable characteristic to this day. She also acquired a knowledge of cooking and handcraft which is very useful.

Big, heavy-set, dark-complexioned Sophia, was fourteen years of age but looked older. Her father, a Russian, dominated the family and looked down on the family of the Puerto Rican mother who spoke little English. Sophia was closely tied to the father who died when she was ten. She had a more attractive older sister and small brother and sister. She hated her mother but was jealous of the love and attention the mother gave the siblings, and she taught them to defy the mother. Sophia was aloof and alone. She decided that she wanted college education so she would be superior to the family. She was sulky, stubborn, rigid, moody, sensitive, resented domination, was easily offended and responded with sarcasm and withdrawal. She did poor work in school. She was sent to a camp of a departmentalized activity type, quite like school. The camp program interested her little, and in an attempt for love and affection she developed a crush on a counselor and threatened suicide.

The next summer, at the age of fourteen, she was sent to *Life Camp.* Early in her stay she said, "This is real camping; the first I've done. I don't like it. I love it." Her rigidity and dignity kept her aloof from the group, but she was outstanding for cooperation, participation and the excellent skills she developed in wood-chopping, sawing, fire-building, etc. She was extremely stoical in matters physical: carrying heavy packs, enduring hot fires, etc. with joy. She said, "I must endure pain. It's something I need to learn." She seemed entirely happy. There were no sex problems apparent. When a group of boys visited, she was not shy but neither was she one of the attention-getting giggly girls.

She said, "I have time. My time will come later." She seemed more mature than the others. She never entered their squabbles, but with a significant look established an understanding sympathy with the counselors when these arose. She talked philosophy with the counselors. She chose Browning and Shakespeare from the camp library. She mentioned the beauty of Vespers and tried to write a poorly expressed article for the camp paper on the beauty of her surroundings.

The next winter she reverted to rigidity and conflict; hostility toward family, poor school work, and finally she turned her aggression against herself, inflicting cuts and burns on her face.

Another summer at camp brought out all the same positive qualities of the preceding summer plus a more outgoing personality and leadership potentialities. Sophia was able to relax and enjoy people, and folk dancing, and express herself more freely in words.

When she reverted again the following winter to the old Sophia of the city, the social agency, basing their judgment on her happy, positive adjustment in camp—as contrasted to her total lack of adjustment in the city—decided to take her out of her home entirely and send her to a boarding school outside the city. Her adjustment there was most favorable and she chose to give up half her next summer's camp experience in order to be with her family a month before returning to boarding school. One of her former public school teachers of the city who had been working closely with the agency and Sophia, visited her in this last summer in camp and wrote the director as follows:

> For the first time in the three years I've known her, she appears radiantly happy. She just seems to belong. She seems sure of herself and shows a sense of security.

While at camp this last summer, because she speaks Spanish fluently, she served as interpreter for the director in showing around a visitor from Uruguay, who was studying camps in North America. Since then, the woman has been corresponding with her and, through her, with the camp director. Sophia gained confidence in herself, pride in the Puerto Rican side of her family, and a mature point of view about camp's handling of the various problems of its children through the insight she gleaned in interpreting the camp program for the director and the visitors. She felt a new importance in camp and a closer relationship to the director and staff.

She wrote to a counselor then with amazing insight for her sixteen years:

> "In 1943 (the year she came to Life Camp) I was like a little ignorant dog who needed love and understanding from a master older than I. Each child has shown and does show his need for attention in a different way, direct or indirect, positive and negative. I think each person does, we all do, don't you think so? We all need attention and affection even more than bread."

At boarding school she has been visiting in the homes of her roommates in their small towns, meeting their friends, going hunting with a gang. She seems happy, returns home at Christmas vacation and gets along rather well with her family. She plans a college education and wants to be a camp counselor.

If camp is to mean more in the lives of campers than a happy vacation or release at the moment, it *must* cause its campers to meet and work out real life situations, and be more ready in attitude and skill to face their problems at home, school and neighborhood. In such a camp some children who have been falsely appearing well-adjusted, even making high marks in school subjects, make poor adjustments. They have been escaping from reality; and were it not for camp, would go on in their little world until, faced with some real difficulty, perhaps as adults, find themselves totally unable to cope with life.

> Pearl was the *school-bright* type—but discovered early that meeting life situations called for more than words. It was her job one day to slice the bread and she was shown a drawer of carving knives of various sizes. The counselor found her a few minutes later, the bread in chunks, while she sawed at it with the one small paring knife in the drawer. She had never been called upon to apply her learning. When confronted with practical situations, she got out of doing the job as often as possible. For prestige in the group, she resorted to *dirty* jokes at which she excelled.

Too often the camp is so organized that the camper uses it only as an escape from reality rather than as a place where he can no longer escape but must face his tasks and, as one parent wrote, "learn to take hold of himself." With a small group of eight campers and two counselors living together day and night, a counselor has much opportunity for observation, discovery of tendencies before they become fixed habits, and for guidance, counsel, and if need be, reference for further help. Good, balanced living with wise observations and therapy usually makes the last named unnecessary, and campers grow into healthful, balanced living.

Hundreds of examples of changes toward good, healthful living could be cited from all camps, but we have space for only a few examples:

> Though Agnes was fourteen years old, it was her first trip away from home and, insecure as she was there, she was so homesick at camp that she spent three weeks of her precious month weeping and pleading to go home, despite all counselor efforts. But in her fourth week something happened, and she wrote of her own free will for the camp newspaper this little article which she entitled: *How I've Changed.* "When I first came to camp, I didn't like it. I was very homesick and was always crying to go home. But later I started to go on hikes, go swimming, etc. I wouldn't even know how to ride a donkey if I hadn't come to camp. I like it now because I learned how to do things I can't do in the city. We took a 12-mile hike to Pole Bridge (the boys' camp). There we climbed a steep hill. Later our counselors took us to a high cliff and we saw such a beautiful view. We saw the Delaware River. Everything was so small! The cars on the road looked like toys. We stayed at Pole Bridge three days and then hiked back. I never realized that the time had flown by and now I have to go back to the city where I can't do any of these things. Now I am so used to camp I hate to go home! It's a wonder how camp can change anyone's mind like that. I can't realize it has happened to me."
>
> Said Pat, "One of the most important things I learned was to have confidence in myself."
>
> Julia: "Being shy with strangers was one thing that I overcame."
>
> Marie: "I learned to have good manners and to eat properly at the table."
>
> After she has happily married, Zelda wrote, "When I look back at the time I spent in camp it seems that I learned almost everything I know in my first five years there, but it took my last year to teach me how to face my problems and how to make friends."

The effect of the out-of-doors on the lives of young campers is enough in itself to make camp urgent for all city children. Such sentences as these are found in their winter correspondence:

> "This past summer at camp seemed to make a great impression on me, as if every little bit of nature had its part in bringing happiness to everybody."
>
> ". . . just to sleep under the stars and moon. I don't think I ever enjoyed anything more."
>
> "Star-gazing and seeing the moon rise over the mountain amazed me beyond doubt and how it shone on the water."
>
> "I can see the beauty of the lake this minute, with the early-morning mist hanging over it like a blanket. Camp has inspired the ideas for several of my poems, and although I am not there now, still does."

Here are two statements from large social agencies of New York City—

> "In these troubled times it is a source of great satisfaction as well as inspiration to note the splendid work and results achieved by your camp in promoting the happiness, well-being, and developing the whole personality of so many children."
>
> "It is from this sort of a family life that Eileen needs the change to camp where she lives with girls with varying background, is taught a better way of living, given a chance to live in the out-of-doors, to be more independent, and exposed to fun, new attitudes, and personalities."

We could multiply them by hundreds such, but need we have more to point the way toward the urgency of camping as part of the rightful heritage and therefore public responsibility in the total education of every child?

CHAPTER XIV

CAMPING FOR TEENAGE PSYCHIATRIC HOSPITAL PATIENTS

Henry K. Kaplan and Robert F. Reneau

Although therapeutic camping for the mentally ill has been used to some extent for more than fifty years, it has recently become increasingly popular and significant. The camp setting, less artificial and exacting than the typical institution, provides an unmatchable therapeutic milieu and enhances the possibilities for self-expression, creativity, and adventure.

At Wisconsin's Mendota State Hospital, an acute treatment and training hospital located in Madison, we have had a camping program for children and adolescents for the past two summers. This year's program is scheduled for late August. Among the hospital's population of 750 patients are 140 patients under 21 years of age. They live in quarters separate from the adults, and most of their regular activities are centered in the building in which they reside.

The activity therapy staff had long looked upon camping as a potentially valuable complement to the therapeutic program for these younger patients. In 1963 we were given an opportunity to use a camp within commuting distance of the hospital, and the staff immediately began planning. In addition to mapping out the practical details involved, we evolved some guiding principles suited to our treatment goals. In essence, our philosophy is a democratic one that encourages individuality, self-expression and responsibility. This is in contrast to a more authoritarian approach, in which a camper's activities are determined by prescription and there is a close adherence to schedule and structure. We feel that our approach emphasizes health rather than sickness.

The chief of activity therapy has found it necessary to share much of the detailed planning with other staff members since this task is in addition to regular duties. The planning has been broken down into the following elements: kitchen and food requirements, selection of campers, recreation equipment, work equipment, orientation of personnel, preparation for emergencies, and readying the camp facilities. This planning must start several months ahead of the camping season.

The camp is located on a lake about thirty miles from the hospital and is surrounded by wooded areas, making such activities as fishing, boating, swimming, and nature study readily available. There is also enough open space for team sports. The camp has a large lodge, with dining area, kitchen, staff living quarters, and infirmary, and two cabins for sixteen occupants apiece. Part of the lodge is used for craft activities. The camp lacks some conveniences, such as plumbing in a few areas, and is in marked contrast to the modern hospital facilities in which the children live. Most of the food preparation is carried on at the camp, but the meals are planned by the hospital dietitian and director of food services, and the food is transported daily from the hospital.

During the first year we held two 3-day camp sessions, one for twenty-two adolescent boys and one for thirteen girls. Last summer these sessions were lengthened to four days, and the groups were enlarged to thirty-five boys and thirty girls. We also held a two-day session for a smaller group of children aged twelve and under.

The children who have taken part in the camping have come from all diagnostic categories. They are selected according to their sense of responsibility and their ability to profit from the experience. There have been exceptions, however, and some poorly functioning children have been included in the hope that the camp experience would encourage remotivation. Some writers feel that the shy, withdrawn child tends to profit most from camping, and we have included children with seclusive behavior. The younger group who took part in the two-day session included some autistic and psychotic children. The ratio of staff to children is increased for this group, so that many of the youngsters have their own staff companions.

The staff members who assist with the camp are selected from those who volunteer to take part. Participation is voluntary in order to attract only those who have an interest in camping and who can comfortably shed many facets of their normal hospital roles. Another reason is that full-time participation in the camp sessions, including sleeping at the camp, means working extra time without additional pay. This has not, to our knowledge, deterred any staff member from taking part.

The camp staff has included activity therapists, nurses, aides, teachers, clerical staff, psychiatrists, psychologists, and social workers. These staff members have taken on duties according to their interests and talents, regardless of their professional positions. The ratio of patients to staff is approximately five to one, and two staff members sleep in each cabin with campers. Medical coverage is provided around the clock.

The short duration of the camping sessions has partly determined the activities and goals we selected. Certainly a program tailored to each child's individual needs with activities planned accordingly has not been attempted.

Each camper has certain obligations for work in his cabin area and for kitchen work, which demand a small portion of his day. Aside from these responsibilities, the campers are free to choose from the activities going on at the time: fishing, canoeing, sailing, hiking, swimming, and other sports. Campers have also been free not to participate, although invariably those who initially refuse soon find themselves active, perhaps in a solitary pursuit or in helping a staff member with a job.

One of the most appealing activities has been clearing the woods of fallen trees. A tornado blew down numerous trees, and this afforded readily available and useful work. It also enabled staff members and campers to work cooperatively, often at opposite ends of a saw. Because the accomplishments of forestry work are measurable, the boys have found this task most gratifying. Most of them have worked enthusiastically and long at it. This is a voluntary activity, unlike the regular chores, which are more like the children's responsibilities in the hospital.

Material incentives and rewards have not been used, but we have been pleased with the enthusiasm shown by the campers who win the banner for the cleanest cabin. It has been especially encouraging to see this reaction in adolescents who have formerly shown only cool detachment toward staff efforts to motivate them.

Following both summer camping sessions we evaluated our reactions to the experience and sounded out our campers for their feelings in order to understand what the camping experience meant to our children. We sought not only to improve the camping program but also to determine what adaptations we can make in the year-round program. We have reached the following general conclusions.

The departure of staff members from traditional roles and uniforms appears to change the way campers perceive them. This permits campers to depart from their patient-role. Thus the opportunity is created for fuller interpersonal relationships and for sensing and dealing with previously shielded aspects of others' personalities. After being known as an impersonal authority figure to a child for many months, a physician might, as the result of several days in the camp environment, emerge as a real person to the child. The changes of setting and roles also seem to facilitate communication between patients and staff. For example, the presence in camp of a staff member's baby resulted in a discussion among a group of girls; they expressed their attitudes toward children and child rearing in a free way seldom attained in the group therapy room. Perhaps the freer interchange is due to the campers' lowering their defenses, which in turn can be traced to the therapist's being more a companion than a therapist.

In our postcamp discussions campers repeatedly commented on their feelings of being trusted, of not being watched, of being *out from under.* And placing greater responsibility on the individual and relaxing controls did result in more responsible, socially acceptable behavior. We have sought within our institution to foster greater responsibility through such practices as letting the children earn privileges, and we certainly have not thought of our child-adolescent program's milieu as a suppressive one. But our children's statements regarding the contrast at camp forced us to look at the pathology perpetuating qualities in their daily institutional existence. We are also mindful, however, of the possibility that a four-day session is little more than an orientation or honeymoon period, and that testing and acting-out behavior could undoubtedly be expected in longer sessions. Such behavior has not arisen, so the working through that might be carried out so well in the camp setting has not been necessary. Therefore, our own experience permits us only to speculate on the efficacy of dealing with problems on the spot rather than in office therapy.

Meaningful work, even without material rewards, appears to be highly important. The camp can in some ways approximate the realities of society more closely than the hospital can, possibly because of the work that must be done. Again, with longer camping sessions we might find it necessary to introduce incentives, but this also could be useful, even essential, to creating a therapeutic and growth-inducing environment.

On the basis of our experience so far, we are quite satisfied with our therapeutic camping program. We don't anticipate any major changes in our approach as long as we continue on a four- or five-day basis. We feel that with longer periods of camping we could capitalize more on forestry or related work and develop the role of cabin counselor. Conceivably we could expand the entire therapeutic program and tie in the camping more closely with our general program goals. For instance a child who has functioned successfully in camping might, upon return to the hospital, join a selected group that has greater freedom and responsibility.

CHAPTER XV

TRAIL CAMPING FOR DELINQUENTS

DELBERT M. KOLE AND HOWARD BUSSE

LAST SUMMER eight groups of twenty to forty teen-age boys and girls adjudged juvenile delinquents were taken on week-long camping trips in the Mount Hood National Forest, about forty miles east of Portland. Unlike many campers, who step off a bus and onto a campgrounds, our groups must hike fifteen miles through rugged mountain terrain from the highway to the permanent campsite. Each camper carries a thirty-pound back-pack containing his own gear. The groups spend three nights on the trail, in sleeping bags sheltered by lean-tos, before arriving at the permanent camp, where they spend two and a half days.

These trips are a major activity of Youth Adventures, a voluntary organization incorporated in 1962 expressly to provide programs and facilities to combat juvenile delinquency in Oregon. An outgrowth of its director's experience in voluntary youth work, YA now has a permanent staff of seven husband-wife teams and four single individuals. Fifteen other paid assistants and more than a hundred citizen-volunteers participate in the camping program. YA is a nonprofit organization sustained primarily by contributions from individuals, churches, social organizations, businesses, and private foundations. Although basically Protestant, YA operates in cooperation with other faiths and provides services without regard to creed or to race.

Since the program began seven years ago, more than 3000 youths have taken part in the camping trips. Most of them were from MacLaren School for Boys and Hillcrest School for Girls, the two state training schools for juvenile delinquents. Others were from the detention halls or parole lists of five county juvenile courts and from two Job Corps centers. One year we included teen-age patients from Oregon State Hospital, but we have since concentrated on delinquent youngsters. However, we believe the activities and principles involved could be used with selected psychiatric patients, providing they are physically fit and able to observe safety rules. Indeed, many of the delinquent youths on the trips have been quite severely disturbed; they were able to participate and benefit, and the volunteer counselors were able to work with them, with staff support and supervision.

Screening of campers varies with the institution. MacLaren excludes boys with serious physical or emotional problems, as well as those heavily engaged in other programs at the school. On the other hand, severely disturbed girls from the maximum-security unit at Hillcrest have been included. In any case, only those who volunteer can go. We usually have twice as many trips for boys as for girls.

Two YA staff men act as directors for the trips; they handle supplies and major disciplinary problems, and plan and supervise the activities on the trail and at camp. On many trips, the wife of one of the trip directors goes along as support for the volunteer staff. A staff member from the school involved serves as observer and adviser. Occasionally a psychiatrist, psychologist, or other professional is invited to come as an observer.

The rest of the staff on the trips are unpaid volunteers who usually give up some of their vacation time to participate; we try to include a doctor or nurse on each trip. The volunteers serve as lay counselors, each supervising a team of five or six campers. Most counselors are parents; many are college graduates working in a variety of fields; they vary widely in their psychological sophistication. Two teen-age boys, also volunteers, are wranglers for the burros. On girls' trips we include teen-age girl volunteers as team helpers; one girl is assigned to each team as a potential confidante and role model.

Before each trip the campers are instructed in using the equipment and observing safety measures. On the morning a trip begins, the campers go by bus to the hike-in point, where they are met by the trail staff. The campers divide themselves into teams and are assigned to a counselor. Each camper is given a backpack in which to carry his own gear; the tents, food, and heavy gear are carried by burros.

The teams start out on the trail about five minutes apart, with the lead team taking the burros. The campsite is reached about 3 P.M., and the teams select their own sites, raise their lean-tos, lay out their sleeping bags, and fix up the area in the hope of earning points for the best campsite of the day. For the rest of the afternoon, the campers have a variety of activities. Each team is encouraged to devise a trail flag, name and song, in order to help develop *esprit de corps* and cooperation among the members. There are also competitive events for which team points are awarded. The campers also prepare a hot meal; dinnertime is 7 P.M.

In the morning, the staff arise at six for a counselor's meeting; the campers are awakened by a rifle shot at seven. Each team cooks its own breakfast, washes the dishes, and packs its gear in time to be on the trail about nine; points are awarded to the team that is the first one ready to leave each day, as well as to the one that collects the most trash along the trail. By the fourth day, the campers arrive at the YA camp, situated by a lake. There each team sleeps in an authentic Indian tepee; the tepees were decorated with Indian designs by Hillcrest girls one winter as another YA activity.

During the week, on the trail or in camp, the teams compete in log-rolling, raft-racing, pole-climbing, rifle-shooting, and hatchet-throwing. Special thrills are provided by building a rope bridge over a rushing river and walking across it, riding the rapids in a rubber boat, retrieving a container of ice cream dropped by parachute from a light plane, fishing for trout, and swimming.

Every evening after dinner the teams gather around the campfire and take turns presenting songs and skits they have composed. Team points and standings are announced, and the winners receive Indian coup feathers to add to their team flagpole; the team with the most feathers at the end of the week wins an airplane ride. The campfire program ends with a brief religion-oriented program in which a staff member gives an informal talk, often a modern-day parable based on his own experiences. Afterward the campers may seek out their counselors or one of the trip directors to discuss any problems they wish.

The typical pattern is for the campers to start out with an air of skepticism. They wonder what the catch is, why anyone is interested in them, and where the limits will be set. Some campers develop a close relationship with their counselors early in the week; others remain aloof and apparently untouched. Some show improvements in attitude and behavior from six to twelve months later and ascribe them to the camping experience.

Invariably on the first day, at least one member on each team tests his counselor, either by threats or by nonparticipation. If the counselor passes the test, by being firm but not domineering, and establishes a climate of mutual respect, the team usually settles down and cooperates. By about the fourth day, many campers have developed sufficient trust in their counselors to begin confiding in them. By the sixth day, when camp breaks up, the parting of many campers and counselors is a tearful event, and some of them continue their relationship later through correspondence and visits.

Reaching that degree of rapport is not always a smooth process, of course. Some of the campers continue to gripe about the food, the amount of work, and other matters. Many counselors, particularly the inexperienced ones, doubt their ability to gain their team's confidence and to control misbehavior. Daily staff meetings are held to deal with such problems, and the trip directors are always available to the counselors.

The counselors are expected to know where to locate each of their team members at any time. The staff use walkie-talkies to keep in contact with one another. On trips where the risk of runaways is usually high, a manned vehicle is occasionally stationed nearby, on a Forest Service road, to overtake any runaways or at least apprehend them at the main highway. The fact that the highway is fifteen miles from camp is in itself a deterrent to elopement attempts, but the major deterrent is peer-group pressure. To date, few campers have attempted to leave, and only four have succeeded. Those who do try to run away are promptly returned to their institution.

Only a few campers have had to be taken back to town for medical attention before the end of camp. Despite the inexperience of most campers and the obvious hazards involved in many of the activities, careful planning and supervision have kept serious accidents to a minimum. Minor injuries and gastrointestinal upsets are common, but they are handled with a well-stocked first-aid kit.

The entire camping experience is designed to carry out principles that have been found effective in reshaping delinquent behavior. They are:

Exposure to nondelinquent models. The volunteer staff consists of teen-agers and adults who have a wholesome outlook on life. The campers not infrequently make open comparisons between the staff and their parents, their friends, and themselves.

Intense small-group interaction. Each team of five or six campers is kept together as a unit in all activities and is in frequent competition with other teams. The only informal mingling with other campers is around the evening campfire. Many teams become tight in-groups, using a high degree of communication and cooperation to accomplish the tasks they undertake.

Focus on specific behaviors. Many of the camp activities have a definite time span, lasting from a few minutes to a few hours, and are the clear responsibility of a certain individual or a certain team. Thus it is easy to gauge performance. Everyone, campers and staff alike, knows who did what, what was expected of them, and how others did on the same or similar tasks.

The point system for competitive activities provides a tangible, detailed record of team performance. It requires each staff member to carefully observe and record his team's actions. He can then use his formal and informal observations in individual or group counseling, which is directed toward helping the campers understand themselves better, become aware of how others see them, and adopt a more acceptable life-style.

Immediate rewards and punishments. The response of peers is probably the most powerful reinforcement of individual behavior. A good cook is appreciated, as is the member whose efforts put his team ahead in a competition. But if a team member refuses to help cook or set up camp, the others must do extra work or go hungry or cold. Thus the team system encourages immediate reactions to positive or negative behavior. The use of team points, which are totaled nightly at the campfire and rewarded with the coup feathers, also provides an incentive for achievement; the teams particularly prize the feathers as tangible evidence of their superiority over other teams.

Effort is rewarded as well as achievement; throughout the week, recognition is given not only to the team with the most points but also to the team and the individual who show the most progress.

Mutual interdependence. The team members must rely on one another for their food, warmth, safety, and social needs, as well as for coup feathers. They must also rely more heavily on the adults for guidance, assistance, and supplies than they do in a more familiar, less isolated setting.

A salient aspect of the program is that many of the activities on the trail are thrilling and potentially dangerous, or at least are made to appear risky. As the Gluecks have pointed out, delinquents have a strong need for adventure.* The campers have many opportunities to display their fearlessness, strength, and superiority in a competitive, constructive framework with tangible rewards. The girls as well as the boys find this appealing. In addition, the inclusion of potentially hazardous activities implies a certain amount of respect for and confidence in the campers' abilities.

Humor is also an important ingredient, and much of it is typical teen-age slapstick. Nothing, including religion and sex, is too sacred to joke about. Humor provides a benign, acceptable method of acting out against authority; by tradition, the trip directors get thrown into the lake at the end of the week.

Underlying all other considerations is the basically religious orientation of the program and the staff. However, traditional religious vocabulary and symbols are carefully avoided. The volunteers are instructed not to push religion, but to make discreet and meaningful use of moments when a youth may be seeking

* Glueck, S. and Glueck, E.: *Unraveling Juvenile Delinquency.* New York, Commonwealth Fund, 1950.

a better understanding of his relationship with man and God. Above all, the volunteers' own attitudes and actions exert a healthful influence on the campers.

Because the staff is voluntary, the campers often regard them as *really caring,* and they feel less need to react against their authority than against that of the institution personnel. The comparative freedom and informality of the camp environment also make the campers less resistant to the staff's influence.

CHAPTER XVI

THERAPEUTIC CAMPING FOR EMOTIONALLY DISTURBED ADOLESCENTS

Tom R. Hobbs and George C. Shelton

Therapeutic camping has been used for some time to deal with emotionally disturbed youngsters, but only recently has it received widespread attention. Several authors have reported successful results in dealing with delinquent* and emotionally disturbed youngsters† by means of fairly long-term and short-term therapeutic camping programs.

We have experienced considerable difficulty and often failure in attempts to deal with hostile-aggressive and withdrawn youngsters with only the across-the-desk 50-minute-hour therapy session. Its weaknesses include the lack of time, lack of carryover from office talk to actual practice, and the reluctance of many youngsters to respond to such an approach. Even weekly group therapeutic activities do not provide the intensive interaction with peers and therapists that such youngsters might benefit from. We therefore decided to explore the therapeutic value of a short-term camping experience with emotionally disturbed adolescent boys attending the outpatient clinic at the Bureau of Mental Health in Birmingham, Alabama.

The campers were members of the clinic's adolescent boys' group, which is composed of ten to twelve youngsters ranging in age from twelve to fifteen years. Their basic and commonly shared problem is one of poor interpersonal relationships with both peers and authority figures. Throughout the year the group

* Blumenthal, L. H.: *Group Work in Camping*. New York, Association, 1947.

† Kole, D.M., and Busse, H.: Trail camping for delinquents. *Hospital & Community Psychiatry, 20*:150, 1969.

meets weekly for two hours with two male counselors in the gymnasium of a local church. At the same time their parents meet in a discussion group in the mental health clinic.

During the adolescents' group sessions, the boys and counselors engage in problem-solving designed to deal immediately with interpersonal problems as they occur, by identifying the problem and discussing alternative means of handling it. In addition, the boys engage in masculine recreational activities such as billiards and basketball. The counselors permit considerable expression of feelings within well-defined limits. The main treatment purposes of the group are to provide adequate male identification figures, guidance in developing and experimenting with new interpersonal skills, and aid in improving self-confidence and motor coordination by means of athletic activities.

Although those weekly meetings have been fairly effective in achieving their goals, it was evident that the boys should be involved in a more intense group experience. Thus we began planning to involve them in a five-day camping and canoe trip during the summer.

When the possibility of the trip was mentioned, the boys eagerly accepted the idea verbally, but as usual were reluctant to sit down and deal with the tasks of planning the details. Because of the small amount of time the boys spent in the program each week, much of the planning had to be done by the counselors. But, the boys were able to help assign camp duties and select menus, and they were receiving training in shelter construction and in safety practices.

START OF THE JOURNEY

After four months of preparation, nine boys and two counselors (the authors), in four canoes loaded with camping equipment, fresh water, and freeze-dried food, began their journey into the backwater wilderness of the William B. Bankhead National Forest in northwest Alabama.

A major purpose of the trip was to confront the boys with the problems of living together cooperatively and being compelled to rely on each other and themselves for survival against nature's odds. To make the adventure as challenging as possible, the canoe safari journeyed into the dense backwoods where no signs of modern civilization existed for miles around. Such wild beauty and adventure seemed to stir emotions of respect and amazement in each boy, coupled with some apprehension about the wisdom of his decision to become involved in such a demanding excursion. For a campsite, the group chose a very primitive area and immediately began unloading the canoes, clearing the brush, setting up shelters (which consisted of 9- by 12-foot plastic tarpaulins for groups of three boys), constructing a latrine, and collecting firewood. This was to be home for five days.

The first two days were hectic, and nature's tranquility was often interrupted by accusations and curses from irritated campers. The initial daily schedule was fairly flexible, and the boys were permitted to engage in any safe activity as long as they did so in groups of three. That arrangement demanded cooperative living and also presented numerous opportunities for both small- and large-group problem-solving sessions. A camper's most frequent means of handling a problem was to appeal to the counselor to exert pressure on an unwilling teammate to conform to the camper's demands. In such instances, the counselor redirected the problem back to the group, and provided guidelines to help in achieving at least a fair level of problem-solving. The primary purpose of the group sessions was to teach new and better methods for handling problems, especially those involving interpersonal conflict.

Such sessions were frequent for the first few days, with the counselor taking a major role in guiding the discussion. However, over the five days of the trip, the small groups as well as the whole group became increasingly able to work out problems with only minimal outside help, although not to a totally adequate level. Many of the boys tried to use the sessions to manipulate the counselor's attention, and he would have to tell them, "Work it out yourselves." Several attempted to end the sessions by offering superficial solutions, but the group was not allowed to break up until the counselors decided that at least some meaningful communication had occurred.

During the first two days, the counselors set examples in cooking, shelter construction, and other camping skills, but gradually decreased their involvement until the boys assumed total responsibility for camp activities. Although the transition was gradual, it was not necessarily smooth. The verbal conflict continued, but the boys began to cooperate better in activities that would eventually benefit the group, such as gathering wood, building fires, preparing meals, and cleaning the utensils afterwards. One reluctant member could break down the chain of interdependence and delay or lose the reward for all; in short, no work, no food. Thus, the boys were being exposed to an environment that demanded team cooperation for survival; group pressure worked very well and conformity to group standards was soon achieved.

ATTEMPTS AT MANIPULATION

The additional responsibilities given to the boys led them to employ the gamut of manipulative techniques with both their comrades and counselors. One boy suddenly developed a painful foot injury that incapacitated him except at mealtime, when he was usually the first in chow line; two boys used strong-arm tactics with their peers to avoid unpleasant tasks; two disappeared whenever work was required; and one was so clumsy, that if he had been home, his parents probably would have intervened and finished the task for him. It was at these times that group pressure was effective. Little authoritative action was required from the counselors, except for frequently and indirectly pointing out an individual's manipulative techniques to the group.

After the first two days, one major organized group activity was planned for each of the remaining three days. The activities usually consisted of canoe trips for various distances, one of which covered twenty miles in eight hours. At these times, *bad* and timid youngsters displayed their best qualities. Considerable physical exertion, determination, and accomplishment showed through exteriors of poor self-concepts and feelings of inadequacy. Pride in accomplishing such feats was obvious. It was indeed inspiring to see a youngster loudly and continually complaining about the exertion required for the trip, but at the same time paddling harder than ever.

Initially, the boys were poor canoe-mates, to say the least. Lack of coordination and cooperation was continual, along with accidental as well as purposeful ramming, swamping, and capsizing. However, the boys' canoeing and camping abilities, as well as their interpersonal skills, improved with the practice demanded by the counselors.

NIGHTLY GROUP SESSIONS

Nightly group therapy sessions were held around the campfire, patterned after Loughmiller's pow-wow.* The events of the day were discussed, both the accomplishments and the disappointments. However, the emphasis was on the campers' feelings toward and ciricism of one another, and their helpful comments about how a teammate might change particular behaviors and maintain others. Those sessions proved to be the highlight of the trip, producing valuable and meaningful communication.

Although the boys seemed to derive a great deal from the sessions once they became involved, they were frequently reluctant to sit down and talk, even after an eventful day of canoing, fishing, swimming, cooking, and hiking. On one occasion, to cope with that problem, the counselors organized a late afternoon canoe trip to a remote area of the lake, where a campfire was built on the lake's edge as nightfall came rapidly. Many of the boys developed doubts about their ability to return to our base campsite at night. However, returning before the next morning was made contingent on the boys' at least trying to participate in the group session, no matter how clumsily or superficially.

After having been given some guidelines, the group arduously produced a number of constructive comments, and meaningful interaction evolved. The boys offered a number of insightful comments about their comrades, and a general atmosphere of good feeling, warmth, and understanding prevailed. Although reluctant at first, they seemed to enjoy the opportunity to express their feelings and opinions to the undivided attention of the group. The session closed with grudges minimized and a feeling of comradeship.

---

* Loughmiller, C.: *Wilderness Road.* Austin, Hogg Foundation for Mental Health, 1965.

Upon embarking for our base campsite, the most insecure and least confident individuals were placed in the first canoe with the only light. Although they requested frequent encouragement and support, they successfully guided the party home and were praised by both campers and counselors. Their pride in themselves as a team was obvious.

Several of the boys matured emotionally during the trip. One example was Danny, who could be described as a very anxious, constricted, *uptight* youngster who had been dominated by a callous stepfather and manipulated by a weak and ineffectual mother. Frequently during the trip, Danny had been goaded and taunted by the older boys of the group, thus reinforcing his very poor concept of himself. With the counselors' encouragement, Danny made several feeble attempts to stand up for himself and to express his emotions, which culminated in a brawl with a strong-arm member of the group. After several minutes, the verbal and physical scuffle was over and Danny was highly praised by the rest of the group, not for fighting but for finally deciding to stand firmly behind his convictions.

The two boys required some time to regain control of themselves, and after they did, the group discussed the reasons and feelings of the combatants. Although the two boys did not emerge as close friends, they seemed to have a greater respect for one another. By way of epilogue, no further conflict occurred between them, and Danny began to display a little more self-confidence and considerably less anxiety.

The camping experience was far less successful for Oliver, a classic product of maternal overprotection who continually griped, whined, and complained, and frequently cried when faced with responsibility. He was adept at manipulating others by "playing dumb" while his teammates carried out his tasks for him. The counselors and the group attempted to prevent such manipulation by meeting his tears with kind firmness and supporting his independent behavior. Even so, the camping experiences, reinforcement techniques, and group pressure were too brief to significantly alter his well-established patterns of coping with stress.

In general, however, most of the boys appeared to benefit from the trip. Although they certainly employed their manipulative skills, they developed some better techniques for handling interpersonal problems, began to operate better as a team, and also developed a greater respect for themselves and their ability to rely on themselves. By the last day, the boys were ready to return home and quickly joined together in cleaning the camp area. Their teamwork was remarkable—no scuffles, and with one exception, no verbal barrages. Upon returning to our point of departure, even the most shy and retiring of them were enthusiastically telling bystanders of their camping adventures. Although they were glad to be home, all the boys displayed pride in having demonstrated their ability to live with and combat nature as a cohesive and vibrant unit.

BENEFITS OF THE TRIP

We feel that such an adventure provides a number of realistic and beneficial conditions for therapeutic intervention. They include:

Exposure to a Challenging but Fairly Well Controlled Environment

The primitive backwoods inherently demand self-reliance, responsibility, and independence in order to acquire even the basic necessities required for comfort, such as food and shelter. In addition, the counselors can construct therapeutic contingencies tailored to suit an individual's particular difficulties.

Equally important is the effect of imitative behavior among the campers, with the counselor serving only as a catalyst and reinforcer. When campers observe the praise received by a fellow member, they may be motivated to act in a way that will elicit a similar response. Furthermore, the susceptibility of children to various influences increases at camp, for they are removed from diverting or diluting influences, such as parental overprotection. Thus the setting affords the counselor considerable environmental control and permits greater opportunity for continuous therapeutic manipulation.

Exposure to an Adventurous Atmosphere Requiring Team Cooperation

Nature provides abundant opportunity for relieving tensions and pent-up hostilities. The camper is exposed to interesting and thrilling outdoor activities and is given the opportunity to try his skills. According to the Gluecks, emotionally deviant youngsters have a strong need for adventure.* Such a setting demands teamwork and intensive interpersonal contact, and although the close-knit living encourages frequent conflict, it also affords opportunity for better communication and practice in resolving conflicts.

Temporary Removal of the Youngster From a Disturbing Environment and Exposure to an Atmosphere That Teaches New and Better Methods of Handling Interpersonal Problems

Because of the teamwork and cooperation required by the counselors, the group had to handle immediately any difficulty arising with any of its members before they could attain a common goal, such as eating dinner after an exhausting day. Thus the boys were motivated to listen to new ideas and to at least attempt some facsimile of problem-solving rather frequently. The nightly group therapy session served to climax each day with a review of the activities, problems, and successes and to provide the boys with feedback about themselves, individually and as a group. The counselors were hopeful that the boys would become able to extend their new-found methods for handling problems to their everyday environment.

Prolonged Exposure to Adequate Adult Models and Increased Time for the Development of Counselor-Boy Relationships

The outdoor camping experience provides a unique atmosphere in which relationships between group members and counselors can grow. Being required to live together twenty-four

---

* Glueck, S., and Glueck, E.: *Unraveling Juvenile Delinquency.* New York, Commonwealth Fund, 1950.

hours a day, coping with a demanding but rewarding environment, encourages group cohesion and more intensive counselor-boy contact. The boys' prolonged exposure to the counselors as models of acceptable, realistic behavior may encourage some degree of identification and imitiation, and may also aid in altering maladaptive attitudes toward authority figures.

Even with so many therapeutic advantages, a camping experience is still plagued to some degree by the perennial troubles of most therapeutic programs—lack of time and the necessity to return the youngster to the same environment that has promoted the difficulty. Following the trip, counselor-parent sessions were held to suggest different modes of handling the more serious problem behaviors and to designate the individual goals for each boy that were initiated and worked toward during the camping trip.

Although most parents said that the youngsters enjoyed and benefited from the trip, a few indicated a change they considered undesirable in their youngster's behavior. For example, Danny, who had been quite anxious, retiring, and self-derogatory, and who had finally stood up for himself during the trip was reported to have become more aggressive with his siblings and peers. His parents, as always, immediately clamped down on any display of aggression, and clinic personnel had to persuade them to allow some expression of socially acceptable and *average* adolescent aggressiveness. Additional guidance for parents was offered in their regular weekly discussion groups, and desirable behaviors in the boys continued to be encouraged in their weekly group meetings.

In retrospect, we believe such therapeutic camping experiences to be of considerable help, providing intense opportunities for close-knit living. Such a program is believed to be a valuable tool for the outpatient treatment of adolescent boys.

CHAPTER XVII

RETARDED CHILDREN AT CAMP WITH NORMAL CHILDREN

NORMAN FLAX AND EDWARD N. PETERS

EARLY EACH YEAR, camp administrators are faced with the task of deciding which children should be accepted in their summer programs. Should the blind, the physically handicapped, the diabetic, the emotionally disturbed, or the retarded child be permitted to join other campers in summer recreation? This question concerns the well-being of both normal and handicapped children.

Dr. Alex Rosen has pointed out:

> The handicapped person cannot be understood merely by analysis of the functional aspects of the handicap alone. Rather, the community's definition of the handicap influences the self-image and social adjustment of the handicapped person. This internalization takes place as the person becomes aware of this societal definition. Thus deviance is established, reinforced, and internalized.*

What, then, should social agencies do about the countless number of low-functioning young people who need service?

While administrators of recreation agencies are becoming increasingly sensitive to the leisure-time needs of the handicapped and the possible effects of rejection on young people seeking inclusion in their programs, they must evaluate the possible effects on other campers of including them, as well as on the scope of their programs. Recent experience of the Jewish Community Centers Association of St. Louis, Mo., with mentally retarded

---

* Rosen, Alex: Theoretical concepts in the behavioral sciences regarding integration. *In* Proceedings of a 1-day institute on integration of the mentally retarded in a community group service agency—a look at knowledge, methods, and gaps. (Meyer Schreiber, ed.) Association for the Help of Retarded Children, New York, N.Y. 1963.

campers suggests some possible approaches to decisionmaking in this regard.

Since the summer of 1966, the agency has placed sixty mentally retarded children in summer camp groups, twenty-nine in day camps and thirty-one in a resident camp. All these children have been diagnosed in the clinical facilities of the St. Louis County Special School District as *educable mentally retarded*, which, according to Missouri State laws, required a measured IQ between 48 and 78; and all have attended special school classes for *educable* retarded children. Most of these children have been in the camping program for several years, some for all four years. The agency's experience with these children has demonstrated that retarded children can participate with normal children in many activities such as swimming, baseball, camp crafts, folk dancing, singing, and work projects. It has also demonstrated that educable retarded children's behavior characteristics fall well within the range of those exhibited by normal children in groups, and that, on the whole, normal children and their parents do not react negatively to having retarded children in camp.

These findings are the results of careful and systematic analysis of information collected in a demonstration project, known as the EMR Project, which was funded by the National Institute of Mental Health.†

Each year the day camp program serves about 1,000 children between the ages of 6 and 14; the resident camp, Camp Hawthorn, serves approximately 420 children each summer between the ages of 8 and 16. Both camp programs are under the direction and supervision of their regular staff members. The EMR Project has its own staff, which includes four trained social workers and a research psychologist.

Beginning with the fall of 1965, whenever an educable mentally retarded child showed an interest in going to camp, a project social worker interviewed both the mother (father) and the child to gain understanding regarding the child's peer relation-

---

† National Institute of Mental Health Project, "Integration of Educable Retardates in Normal Groups," Grant No. MH-14424. Co-sponsored by the Jewish Community Centers Association of St. Louis, Mo., and the Social Science Institute of Washington University, St. Louis, Mo. (NSF grant No. G-22296.)

ships both in school and in the neighborhood, learn about his interests and areas of skill, and obtain information about his handicaps, both visible and hidden. The social worker also reviewed each child's social history, psychological diagnosis, and school experience as noted in the special school records.

Following this intake procedure, the social worker then made a general assessment of the child and attempted to predict the degree of success the child would achieve at camp. Each child was rated on a 1 to 5 scale, which was the worker's judgment of his social readiness. The five point scale had the following definitions: (1) unsuited–to be rejected for camp; (2) marginal–could be given camping opportunity only if an especially appropriate group of children could be located for him; (3) a fair risk–probably could obtain at least partial success, but would require a great deal of help; (4) a good risk–probably could succeed in any one of several camp groups; and (5) an excellent risk–likely to find personal satisfaction, likely to be accepted by other campers, and likely to be an asset to group life. Unless judged unsuited, the child was placed in a group, which in the judgment of the staff, afforded him the best chance for success.

To help the research staff learn how the children performed in their camp groups, each counselor filled out a Group Participation Form on the retarded child in his group. Designed to measure the child's degree of participation in group life, the form included thirty-four items concerned with specific types of behavior in specific situations. Most of the questions had to do with the frequency with which the child behaved in the way described or with the way he behaved most frequently in a particular situation. For example, one question was, "Does this [group] member require frequent and/or continuing reminder of procedures and/or rules?" In answer, the counselor was required to check *always, usually, sometimes, seldom,* or *never.* Another item asked the counselor to check the response that best described the child's most frequent way of contributing to the group's decision about what to do. The form listed five choices for this item:

1. Wanders off from the group during planning.
2. Physically present, but makes no contribution.

3. Contributes suggestions or questions that are usually irrelevant or unrelated.
4. Contributes some relevant suggestions or questions.
5. Takes leadership in suggesting the ideas that are adopted.

Before using the form to assess the group adjustment of the mentally retarded campers, the project requested more than a hundred counselors to use the form to assess the behavior of other children in their groups, selected at random. This precaution was taken to prevent a characteristic of a retarded child's behavior from being attributed to his retardation when a normal child might exhibit the same type of behavior.

A statistical analysis of these forms indicated that the Group Participation Form was collecting information primarily on three dimensions of a child's participation in the group: (1) the amount of aggressive acting-out behavior exhibited by the child in the group; (2) the extent to which the child seemed to belong to and feel comfortable in the group; and (3) the extent to which the child directed his attention and interaction toward the counselor. Each of these dimensions could be measured for each child by combining the child's scores on pertinent items on the form. The three sets of items selected for this purpose were labeled the Aggressive Acting-Out Scale, the Belongingness and Comfort Scale, and the Leader Orientedness Scale.

The Aggressive Acting-Out Scale assessed the frequency of various kinds of acting-out behavior, such as (1) the extent to which the camper argued and fought with the counselor, (2) how often he became aggressive when faced with derogatory or deflating remarks or with failure, and (3) how much he bragged and boasted, bullied or dominated, disrupted the group, or sought attention. When the measures of these items were combined, the result was a fairly accurate measure of the extent of aggressive acting-out behavior the camper exhibited in the group.

The Belongingness and Comfort Scale assessed the degree of the child's involvement in the group's activities, the extent to which he tended to withdraw from other children, the degree to which other children chose or accepted him, and the degree of comfort he seemed to feel in new or strange group situations. The combined scores on these items measured the degree to which the child had socially adapted or *made it* in the group situation.

The Leader Orientedness Scale was composed of items describing how much the child tended to direct various kinds of interaction and verbalization toward the group leader.

Further statistical analysis has indicated that the three scales are all fairly reliable, consistent measures of uniform, distinct dimensions of children's behavior in groups.

SOME FINDINGS

Group Participation Forms were collected on every mentally retarded child in a camp group and on a randomly selected normal member in each camp group containing such a child, after the child had spent one full day at camp and again at the end of the camp session. The scores on each of the three scales were analyzed to determine if there were any consistent differences, on the average, between the mentally retarded children and the normal group members or if there were any consistent differences, on the average, between the children's behavior early in the camp session and at the completion of camp. These analyses showed no marked differences, on the average, between the retarded and the normal children in the amount of aggressive acting-out behavior or in the amount of leader oriented behavior.

However, the Aggressive Acting-Out Scale showed that all campers, retarded and of normal intelligence, tended to act out more at the end of the camp session than at the very beginning. This will not be a surprise to persons who have ever worked with children in camp groups. However, it does indicate the project's measure of aggressive acting-out behavior is sensitive enough to pick up this difference in an objective, quantifiable manner.

The Belongingness and Comfort Scale showed a distinct difference between the scores of the mentally retarded children and the scores of the children regarded as normal: on the average, the mentally retarded children scored much lower than the other campers. However, while the difference in average scores was large, the scores of the mentally retarded children ranged from a high that is well above the average score of the other campers down to a low that is well below the scores of most of the other campers. Thus, we have an objective and quantified measure of what is already apparent from casual observation of educable mentally retarded children in camp groups—that, in general, these children are not as much at ease as other campers, but there are wide individual differences among them. Some mentally retarded children do as well in camp groups as many other campers.

That some mentally retarded children can apparently fit well into some groups of normal children makes any blanket policy against placing mentally retarded children into normal camp groups unreasonably rigid. However, some improvement is needed in the ability to predict which mentally retarded children can be integrated into camp groups with normal children with a relatively high degree of success. The Belongingness and Comfort Scale, in providing a relatively sensitive and objective measure of the extent to which a camper adapts socially in his camp group, makes it possible to explore the extent to which various kinds of information are useful for predicting how a mentally retarded child will get along in camp.

The social worker's general assessment of each mentally retarded child who applied for camping, mentioned in the beginning of this article, was an attempt to predict the degree of success each would have in integrating into a camp group on the basis of the information obtained by the social worker during the intake procedure. These predictions, however, were subjective judgments. They did not stand up, under post-camp statistical analysis, as valid predictions of which mentally retarded children would do better than other mentally retarded children in fitting into a camp group.

However, in addition to giving a general assessment or *global prediction* for each mentally retarded child, the social worker rated each child on forty characteristics from information obtained in the intake procedure. Of these forty characteristics, eight have turned out to be related to the success of the educable mentally retarded children in camp groups as measured by the Belongingness and Comfort Scale, and the social worker's rating on them to be much closer to a valid prediction of the children's degree of success at camp. The eight characteristics are: (1) the amount of neighborhood street play the child participates in; (2) his awareness of the needs of others; (3) his ability to delay appropriate gratification; (4) his ability to follow directions; (5) the extent of his skill in playing highly organized games and also (6) his skill in playing unorganized games; (7) his gross motor coordination; and (8) his overall personal appearance.

That each of these characteristics should be related to how well a child gets along in a camp group is not surprising. What is interesting is that some of the information that can be acquired about a mentally retarded child through the intake procedure does help to predict whether the child may become a comfortably participating member of a camp group. The extent to which an educable mentally retarded child plays with normal children in his neighborhood is probably the best single indicator of whether or not he is likely to adapt socially to a camp group. In other words, if he can *make it* in his neighborhood, he can probably *make it* at camp.

The other characteristics that are predictive of successful adaptation to camp probably also influence the mentally retarded child's ability to integrate into neighborhood play groups. Mentally retarded children who can participate in camp activities, because they are relatively skilled at playing games, have relatively good coordination, and can follow directions, will probably get along better socially than mentally retarded children who do not have the ability to participate in such activities. Also, those mentally retarded children who are sufficiently stable emotionally to be aware of the needs of others and to be able to delay gratification appropriately will probably get along with normal campers better than children who do not possess these qualities.

OTHER MEASUREMENTS

Nonparticipant observers provided another measure of how well the mentally retarded children did in camp. In the summers of 1968 and 1969, the staff of the project took part in nonparticipant observations at camp. Each mentally retarded child and the normal child selected as his control were observed twice during camp activities, including archery, soccer, swimming instruction, gathering wood for campfires, bicycle rides, folk dancing, free time, storytelling, making ice cream, and eating lunch. The staff rated each child's degree of (1) involvement in activity, (2) apparent pleasure in the activity, and (3) understanding of the activity. The analysis of these observations showed that retarded children were just as involved in activities as normal children and exhibited more apparent pleasure during activities than the normal children. The normal children, however, were rated as apparently understanding activities better than the mentally retarded children.

The counselors' observations of the children's social adjustment were also considered important. For four summers—1966 through 1969—on the last day of each session a form called the Social Adjustment Form was given each counselor, with these instructions:

> "It is assumed that some children seem to adjust, generally speaking, better than others. We would like to get your impression about the relative social adjustment of the children in your group. Please rank members in order of their adjustment."

A total of ninety-three Social Adjustment Forms were collected from camp groups that included mentally retarded children. There was some overlapping since some of the children attended more than one camp session or went to camp more than one season. On these forms, mentally retarded children were ranked above their normal controls twenty-five times and below sixty-eight times. Only on thirty-two of the ninety-three forms were mentally retarded children ranked the lowest in their camp groups.

There was a notable relationship between the children's social adjustment ranking and their ratings on the Belongingness and Comfort Scale in the Group Participation Form. The higher the child was ranked on the Social Adjustment Form, the higher was his belongingness and comfort score.

STAFF REACTIONS

How do the camp director, the camp supervisors, and the counselors feel about including retarded children in camp?

In the fall of 1968, the project sent a questionnaire to ninety-five staff members of resident and day camps, including counselors, camp directors, and supervisors, to ascertain their reactions to the research demands, their attitudes about including mentally retarded children in the camp, and their assessment of the interaction between the mentally retarded children and the other children. Sixty-four questionnaires were returned.

Seventy percent of the responding staff members complained that the research demands were time-consuming. Nevertheless, twenty-one of the twenty-four camp administrators and twenty-three of the thirty-five counselors responding to this question said they would like to have a retarded child in their group or lodge if they were to return to camp. Of twenty-four supervisors, sixteen reported that they felt that the research component at camp enhanced their jobs professionally.

Thirty-one of the thirty-nine counselors reported that having mentally retarded children in their groups made them more sensitive to the problems of other campers. Half the counselors reported that the retarded children had been no more difficult than the other children, but did require more of the leader's time.

The great majority of the responding camp staff members reported feeling that the camping experience was beneficial to the mentally retarded child. Of the sixty-four respondents, forty-four reported that the other children did not pick on the mentally retarded children, or only did so to a minor degree; and fifty-four reported that the mentally retarded children did not pick on the other children, or only to a minor degree. To the question, "What do you consider the major behavior problem at camp?" sixty of the sixty-four replied "emotional disturbance." Only three replied "mental retardation." Eighteen of the thirty-nine counselors responding to this question suggested that there were educable mentally retarded children at camp who should not have been accepted.

More than half the counselors reported feeling that the other children had a better camp experience because the educable mentally retarded children were included. None of the counselors said they would refuse to return to camp because of its participation in the project. Most of the camp staff members said they felt that additional precamp training would have been of value in helping counselors meet some of the special needs of the mentally retarded children.

One supervisor's statement conveys the attitude that seems to have been prevalent throughout the program:

> In most cases the retarded children were indistinguishable from the other children, that is, the other children in the group usually did not recognize that their group included a mentally retarded member. I wholeheartedly approve of their attending camp with normal children.

Another supervisor wrote:

> Having educable mentally retarded children at camp was a most beneficial experience for all counselors and campers.

A counselor reported:

> This is not a very comprehensive survey because I had two completely different mentally retarded children. They behaved differently and affected the group differently.

Another counselor said:

> The inclusion of mentally retarded children gave the normal kids an opportunity to learn about some of the troubles mentally retarded children have and to be understanding and patient.

And still another counselor wrote:

> More people should be made aware of the capabilities of the educable mentally retarded child. I for one realize that they can and should be treated as any other member of the group.

But there were also negative responses. One camp staff member reported:

> My personal experience with a mentally retarded child was a very trying one, for which I was drastically unprepared. In most of the problems that arose, I found that my only solution was to hand the mentally retarded child over to my supervisor.

Another respondent was doubtful:

> In most cases, I don't think the counselors or junior counselors are able to understand a mentally retarded child because they have not been educated in this area. Did we really help the retarded child?

And one counselor reported:

> If the groups were smaller, then more attention could be given to the mentally retarded child.

OTHER CHILDREN AND PARENTS

What about the reactions to the mentally retarded children of the other children in the camp and their parents? Staff members of the project interviewed a normal child and one of his parents from forty-four camp groups that had included a mentally retarded child. Of the forty-four children interviewed, 75 percent (33) had positive reactions to the camp experience. In fact, thirty-eight out of forty-four returned to the agency's program the following winter or re-enrolled for camp the next summer. Of the forty-four parents interviewed, 85 percent (37) gave no indication of having objections to the Center's continuing the policy of integration. The parents' reactions generally concurred with their children's. In twenty-five instances both parent and child reacted positively to the inclusion of the mentally retarded child. In eight instances the child reacted negatively to the mentally retarded child but the parent reacted positively. In three instances the parent had negative reactions, but the child either definitely liked the mentally retarded child or did not regard him as different from the other children in his group. In only five instances did both parent and child react negatively to the mentally retarded child.

IN CONCLUSION

The EMR Project has demonstrated that many educable retarded children, when given the opportunity, can participate successfully in camp activities with normal children. The statistical findings suggest the characteristics a mentally retarded child might need in order to become a part of a group. In reality, however, retarded children showing a wide range of different characteristics have integrated adequately into the camp groups. Of the sixty retarded children enrolled in camp groups in 1969, only five children were unable to complete a session started. As one counselor reported:

> The mentally retarded children had many of the same behavior problems as the so-called campers. Some were cooperative, some were not; so generalizations are almost impossible.

For evaluative reasons, this project included only those retarded children who were *educable.* This does not mean to imply, however, that some *trainable* retarded children (IQ's 25 to 48) might not under favorable circumstances get along with normal children in a camp group. Occasionally a child from a class for *trainable* children has participated in other activities sponsored by our agency.

Often one experience is not sufficient to judge a child's eventual success; he needs to be evaluated over time. It behooves recreational agencies, therefore, to open their facilities to retarded children—some of the loneliest members of our society—to give them insofar as possible the same opportunities that are afforded other children in the community.

APPENDIX

THE FOLLOWING SOURCES of additional information and reference are provided for those planning programs in the fields of camping and therapeutic recreation.

ASSOCIATIONS

American Camping Association
Bradford Woods
Martinsville, Indiana 46151

National Campers and Hikers Association
7172 Transit Road
Buffalo, New York 14221

Association of Private Camps
55 West 42nd Street
New York, New York 10036

National Camping Association
353 West 56th Street
New York, New York 10019

National Therapeutic Recreation Society
1700 Pennsylvania Avenue, N.W.
Washington, D.C. 20006

BOOKS

Cheney, Theodore: *Camping by Backpack and Canoe.* New York, Funk & Wagnalls, 1970. $7.95

Riviere, Bill: *Backcountry Camping.* Garden City, Doubleday, 1971. $6.95

Saijo, Albert: *The Backpacker.* San Francisco, 101 Publications, 1972. $1.95

Shivers, Jay: *Camping—Administration, Counseling, Programming*. New York, Appleton-Century-Crofts, 1970. $7.95

Sunset Editors: *Sunset Camping Handbook*. Menlo Park, Lane, 1970. $1.95

PERIODICALS

Camping. The Galloway Corporation, 5 Mountain Avenue, North Plainfield, New Jersey 07060. $7.50 per year.

Camping Guide. Rajo Publications, Inc., 319 Miller Avenue, Mill Valley, California 94941. $5.00 per year.

Backpacker Magazine. Quarterly. 28 West 44th St., New York, New York 10036. $10.00 per year.

AUTHOR INDEX

L

M

N

O

P

R

S

T

V

W

SUBJECT INDEX